THE MAKING OF AN
EXHIBIT HALL

BRINGING TO LIFE
AMAZONIAN INDIAN CULTURE

ROBERT L. CARNEIRO

Curator Emeritus of South American Ethnology
American Museum of Natural History

authorHOUSE®

AuthorHouse™
1663 Liberty Drive
Bloomington, IN 47403
www.authorhouse.com
Phone: 1 (800) 839-8640

Published by AuthorHouse 08/15/2019

ISBN: 978-1-7283-2245-2 (sc)
ISBN: 978-1-7283-2244-5 (e)

Library of Congress Control Number: 2019911323

Print information available on the last page.

Dedication

To Laila Williamson,
Full partner in this endeavor and faithful
friend for, lo, these many years.

When I began working at the American Museum of Natural History in September, 1957, I knew I had inherited two projects. One was to carry out field work in the Peruvian Montaña, doing what my predecessor, Harry Tschopik, had envisioned doing but had died before he could do so. This project I was able to accomplish within my first five years at the Museum.

The second project, though, took a bit longer—nearly three decades longer. This second project was the re-installation of the South American exhibit hall.

A few years before my arrival at the Museum there had been an old South American hall but it had begun to show its age before I got here and had been closed down. During its later days, once it was no longer open to the public, the windows of the hall, which looked west onto Columbus Avenue in mid-Manhattan, had been covered over with brown paper.

Some of the exhibits had actually remained in place before the final closing, and I remember seeing them shortly after arriving at the Museum. Still in place was an exhibit whose old fashioned look betrayed its age. One of the cases, as I recall, had row upon row of virtually identical polished stone celts from the West Indies. Little or no information was given about how they were made or what they were used for.

After its final closing the South American hall became something of a junk room, the repository of such oddments as an old dentist's chair. (I never did learn how such a thing wound up there.)

But the direct ancestor of the new South American hall which we were to embark upon was not the old hall but a temporary exhibition—still standing when I came to the Museum—called "Men of the Montaña." This exhibit had a very convoluted history which is worth taking the trouble to recount. And to do so we must go back to the time of the Second World War.

In the first months of that war the Japanese overran southeast Asia, among other things cutting off the U.S.' source of rubber, which was essential to waging the war the U.S. was now engaged in. Since southeast Asia was no longer accessible, an alternate source of rubber had to be found. And that meant Amazonia, where it was first discovered that a certain tree, *Hevea brasiliensis,* on being tapped, yielded a thick sap—latex—which could be processed into rubber.

But as long as rubber trees grew far apart—as they did in Amazonia—and not close together as they did on plantations, rubber production was bound to be limited.

Actually, growing rubber trees on plantations had been tried in Amazonia by Ford and Firestone, but both attempts had failed. A leaf blight that readily spread from tree to tree doomed the experiment. Rubber trees introduced into southeast Asia in the late 19th century and grown on plantations had somehow escaped the leaf blight. Southeast Asian plantations thrived and rubber could be produced in abundance.

But now Amazonia had to be turned to by the U.S. as the only available source, and its rubber production had to be stimulated.

In an effort to accomplish this the Rubber Development Commission was formed. In charge of it was put a wealthy Wall Street businessman named Francis Adams Truslow, who had been head of the New York Curb Exchange. Truslow went to Amazonia, traveled widely while he was there, and talked to many small rubber tappers, encouraging them to maximize their production of latex.

In the course of his travels in the Amazon Truslow met Raúl de los Ríos who for years had been in the Guardia Civil stationed in the rainforest area of Peru. De los Ríos had begun collecting artifacts from the Indian tribes he encountered and eventually amassed an impressive collection of their material culture. Altogether it amounted to several thousand artifacts.

Seeing that de los Ríos' collection was not only large but of high quality, Truslow decided that it belonged in a major museum. And being from New York, it was no surprise that he thought it should be the American Museum of Natural History. He bought the de los Ríos collection and donated it to the American Museum with the understanding that a significant portion of it should be displayed in a temporary exhibition.

The task of setting up this exhibition fell to Harry Tschopik, Curator of South American Ethnology. Harry's field experience, extensive as it was, had been entirely in the Andes with Aymara-speaking peoples. He had no particular familiarity with the culture of the Indians of the rainforest, just east of the Andes.

Nevertheless, it was his job to mount what turned out to be a major exhibition.

To prepare himself for the assignment, Tschopik turned to the mammoth *Handbook of South American Indians* which was then the principal source of information on the culture of the Indians of Amazonia, including the Peruvian rainforest. Harrry quickly mastered what he needed to know in order to carry out the work which lay ahead of him. When it finally opened, the temporary exhibit was called "Men of the Montaña"—"Montaña" being the term applied to the area of rainforest from which the de los Ríos collection had come.

The exhibition was installed in a gallery that had been used for short-term temporary exhibits. And when "Men of the Montaña" opened to the public in November, 1952, it was scheduled to run for five months. But it ended up running for 22 years, a measure of its popularity. And it finally closed only to give way to a new permanent exhibit hall on the peoples of Asia.

"Men of the Montaña" placed on exhibit artifacts never before seen in New York. It received critical acclaim as well as enjoying great popular success. The exhibit also made use of new exhibition techniques including some clever ones. For example to simulate the sound of a tropical rain storm it was found that holding a plastic shower curtain under a shower nozzle running at full force produced a sound that seemed more like a rain storm than did the actual thing.

Finally, after two decades during which "Men of the Montaña" was viewed by many thousands of visitors, it was gone. But its success gave us reason to believe that the public was ready for its successor, a hall that would present a fuller and deeper picture of the culture of the native peoples of South America than could be found anywhere else. The new hall would include archaeology as well as ethnology, since our collection of Peruvian antiquities probably excelled that of any other museum in the this country.

The anticipation we felt made us eager to begin work on the new hall.

Actually, an abortive attempt to work on the new hall had been made back in the late 1960s, coinciding with the Museum's early preparations to celebrate its one hundredth anniversary. Junius Bird, then Curator of South American Archaeology, and I began drawing preliminary sketches of what we wanted the new hall to look like, Junius working on the archaeological part and I on the ethnological part.

But nothing came of it since the City's financial crisis intervened and put a stop to any serious work on the hall.

Although technically the Museum is a private institution, the buildings are owned by the City of New York, and thus any major architectural changes that have to be made in them, such those often entailed by a new exhibit hall, had to be paid for out of the City's capital budget. And at that point the city's funds for such changes had run dry.

Still, the false start we had made did not go for naught. I had made half a dozen sketches of what I thought the layout of the ethnological section of the hall should look like, and I'm sure Junius had done the same for his section.

I have always felt a bit uncomfortable on entering an exhibit hall for the first time and not knowing which way to proceed; that is, which direction the curator who designed the hall intended for me to go in order to get the best grasp of the narrative he meant to convey. I made up my mind that someone entering my section of the hall would not be left in a quandary on that score. Still, directing the visitor's route had to be done subtly, without hitting him over the head ... without having an arrow reading "COME THIS WAY."

At that time, though, my "philosophy of exhibit design" was still rudimentary, not having evolved much beyond this point.

However another consideration bore in on me, namely, that in designing the new hall I would have a limited amount of space to work with. Of the 8,000 square feet in the standard exhibit hall at the American Museum only half would be assigned to me for the ethnological part, the other half being reserved for Craig Morris' South American archaeology section (Craig having succeeded Junius Bird in that capacity). That meant that I had at my disposal some 4,000 square feet in which to accommodate what turned out to be close to a thousand artifacts. My work, as I saw it, would thus have to be an exercise in compression: how to pack a relatively large number of objects into a restricted space and do so most effectively.

This eventuality seemed not to be very pressing when considered in the abstract. But then something happened that forced my hand. I had to start thinking about it concretely, if not urgently.

On January 20, 1980 planning the South American hall went from neutral into high gear. Tom Nicholson, director of the Museum, received word—which he quickly passed on to Craig and me—that the City had found enough money in its capital budget for us to start working on the South American hall. Thus plans that for so long had been held in abeyance suddenly had to spring to life.

* * * *

Shortly after Tom had given Craig and me the welcome news he announced that before we began to make definite plans for the hall he wanted to take us to Berlin to see what he considered the best exhibit of native South American Indian cultures in any museum in the world. The exhibit he meant was in the Ethnological Museum in west Berlin.

Craig and I were, of course, only too glad to go on this trip and take a look at the exhibit Nicholson praised so highly. At this stage our ideas for our hall were still pretty fluid, not nearly so fixed that we were not ready to entertain new ideas from whatever source they came.

Besides, I had never been in Berlin. At that time—1980—the city was still divided into an eastern and western sector, with the infamous wall dividing the two.

We arrived in Berlin on a Sunday afternoon in February and registered at the Kampinsky Hotel at $92 a night, an amount which in those days seemed to me exorbitant. But since the Museum was paying the bill ....

We arrived in Berlin early enough to be able to have dinner out at a fine restaurant. I happen to be very fond of sauerbraten which I had often enjoyed at a local German restaurant in Riverdale, where I lived. Thus I was looking forward to experiencing what that dish was like in a *real* German restaurant.

What a disappointment!

The sauerbraten in that restauant was nowhere near as tasty as what I was used to having in New York.

The next day was Monday and we were all set to go to the Ethnological Museum in Dahlem, west Berlin, to see the vaunted South American exhibit. But it turned out that the Ethnological Museum was closed on Mondays, so we went on a busman's holiday, visiting another museum in Berlin instead. It was the Pergamon Museum of classical antiquities, which was right in the heart of the city.

Like most everyone interested in art I was familiar with the bust of the beautiful, slim-necked Queen Nefertiti, which appears in so many histories of art, but I had no idea in what museum it was to be found. I soon found out. It was in the Pergamon Museum which we were about to visit.

There she was, in a small exhibit case by herself. But when I finally laid eyes on her my reaction was one of shock. As many times as one has seen photographs of her sculpted likeness, she is always shown in profile, never from the front. Moreover, it has always been her right side that is shown, never her left. Why? Because one day in the distant past some vandal gouged out her left eye.

The desecration is there for all to see—if you look at her from the front. That is why she is never photographed from that angle.

The next day the Ethnological Museum was open and we were there bright and early. The exhibit hall Tom wanted us to see was there, and it was indeed a good one. Only Tom didn't have it quite right. It was not an exhibit of native South American cultures but of the cultures of the Pacific. They were indeed displayed in a very spacious exhibit hall—spacious enough to be able to hold five or six dugout canoes—spaciousness to be envied since we didn't have space to exhibit for even one.

On the other hand the hall of Mesoamerican archaeology, one floor above the Pacific hall, was actually the one Tom should have steered us to because it made extensive use of Hahn exhibit cases, which he had decided were the ones we would be using. And there was reason for his being so insistent on it.

Back home the new Asia hall, which was now nearing completion, had caused no end of trouble. The guest curator for that hall, Walter Fairservis, had had exhibit cases built expressly for that hall, but for some reason they had proved unsatisfactory and had had to be ripped out and replaced, at great expense. Tom had vowed then and there that the same misadventure would not occur in our hall. Like it or not, he said, we would use the modular Hahn cases he had chosen, already built and ready to install. But at least he assured us that they were the best cases of their kind to be found anywhere I neglected to mention earlier that also along on this trip was Eugene Bergmann, the designer whom George Gardiner, the head of the Exhibition department, had assigned to work with us on the South American hall. Gene stayed behind in Germany after we left in order to make a side trip to Frankfort where the Hahn cases were manufactured. There he hoped to familiarize himself with the cases, especially with the advantages they offered the designer of an exhibit hall. I will have more to say about these Hahn cases later.

Two other things happened on that trip to Berlin that have remained in my mind.

In the store rooms of the Ethnological Museum I got to see some of the artifacts collected by Karl von den Steinen in the Upper Ximgú in central Brazil when he made that region known to the world on his expedition of 1884. Seeing the objects he had brought back from that region was particularly meaningful to me since I did my first ethnographic field work in that same egion a little more than half a century after von den Steinen discovered it.

The other recollection from that trip was of a far different sort. It was waking up in the middle of the night and hearing, for the first and only time in my life, the earie song of what nust have been a nightingale perched on the ledge outside my hotel window.

*   *   *   *

Properly energized, Craig and I returned to New York, eager to start work on our sections of the South American hall. Still, many hurdles remained to be surmounted before we could actually begin working in earnest.

To begin with, the Museum administration had decided that there would no longer be exhibits on the fourth floor on the west side of the Museum. Henceforth that space would be devoted solely to store rooms and offices. Furthermore the exhibits already located in that part of the building would have to be moved to some other location. For starters that meant that the recently completed Pacific hall, designed by Margaret Mead (now deceased) had to relinquish its present location and come to occupy new quarters.

At this point I must inject a little more history into this narrative. The space that the new South American hall was to occupy was exactly the same space it had occupied in its previous existence—that is, on the second floor of the Museum on the west side of the building. On the third floor, directly above the old South American hall, had been the old Philippine hall. It was an old style hall, which it showed its age (among other ways) by the fact that, in the center of it the floor was pierced by a large well through which the visitor could look down into the South American hall. The existence of this well meant, however, that the potential exhibit space in that hall was severely curtailed.

On the fourth floor, directly above the old Philippine hall, was the new Pacific hall which, although only recently completed, had to vacate its location. This was because of the Museum administration's recent edict about removing all exhibits from that sector of the building. The new place for the Pacific hall was be one floor down from its old quarters, that is, to where the Philippine hall had been. Thus the new location of the Pacific hall would be directly above where the new South American hall—our hall— was to be.

And since the Pacific hall as it stood was a full-sized hall, and had to be fitted into the space of the old Philippine hall, the well in the center of that hall had to be eliminated and floored over. This would greatly enlarge the space available for exhibits in the relocated Pacific hall.

Keep in mind that the floor of the new Pacific hall was also to be the ceiling for our hall. Laying down the new floor above us would be a major undertaking which would keep us from doing any work in our hall until after it was completed.

The new flooring, since it had to cover over a large opening, would be of great weight. So heavy in fact that to support it huge I-beams would have to be introduced into the building and placed over the tops of the structural columns in our hall. These I-beams were so large that the only way to get them into the Museum was to breach the outer walls of the building and then insert them through the opening thus created.

I cannot vouch for the way this was done but It was said at the time that at a certain stage of the opeeration the Museum's outer walls were actually broken through. In retrospect I find it hard for mr to believe that several large sandstone blocks forming the Museum's outer walls were actually dislodged to permit this to be done. Yet somehow the big I-beams had to be gotten in, and they were.

In any event, this did not pose a problem for us. In fact we welcomed the interruption since it gave us more time to work on certain preliminary work that has to be done. And there was plenty of it.

When I speak of "us" I am referring to Laila Williamson, my scientific assistant, and myself. Initially I expected to have several assistants assigned to help in carrying out the installiation of the hall. In the end, though, it didn't work out that way. Laila and I did all the curatorial work ourselves. And it turned out for the better. With just two people involved in this aspect of it, the work was streamlined and simplified.

And here let me put into print what I have told others more than once, including in her presence. By now she may be tired of hearing it but I am not tired of saying it: Were it not for Laila, the hall would have taken twice as long to complete and would not be half as good.

Our job at this stage, while we waited for the architectural changes to be made and the new Hahn cases to be installed, was to go through the four store rooms of Amazonian artifacts from which we were to select those that would ultimately fill our exhibit cases.

It was a two-step process. First, we had to pick out what we considered to be candidates for exhibition. The next step, after we completed the first one, was to choose from among them the specimens that would eventually go into the exhibit cases.

We did not have any hard and fast criteria for making the initial selections. Just some rules of thumb that we had in mind as we handled the objects, one after another. We wanted artifacts that were in good condition but at the same time that showed signs of having been used. We avoided objects so pristine in appearance that we suspected they might have been made to trade, especially to tourists and to not-yet-experienced anthropologists.

I had learned from experience while arranging trades with the setting up exchanges that Amazonian Indians are not above trying to palm off something they know to be subpar, figuring they can get away with it.

I remember in particular hearing the Amahuaca joke among themselves— thinking I couldn't understand them— about a wooden mortar I had commissioned someone to make for me which, when the object was finally presented to me as finished was of such poor quality that I accepted it only to get rid of it at the first opportunity.

*   *   *   *

Let me pause here to provide some idea of the range of artifacts Laila and I had to choose from. Given its name, you would expect the South American hall to include artifacts made from anywhere in the entire continent, from the Isthmus of Panama to Tierra del Fuego. But that was not the case. From the start there was the constraint that Laila and I would be dealing only with ethnographic material (more correctly, *ethnological* material). Archaeology was not our concern—that was the province of Craig Morris, who had succeeded Junius Bird as Curator of South American Archaeology. Craig and I each would deal only with that half of the collections that pertained to our specialties and our sections of the hall. We worked together harmoniously but independently. Craig arranged the archaeological half of the hall in whatever way he chose to, and I did the same with my half. We ran along parallel but separate tracks.

The one exception was when we were laying out the arrangement of the anterior part of the hall (Section 6) which, being an introduction to the entire hall, turned out to be a mixture—a mish-mash, actually—of ethnology and archaeology. Here Craig and I had to cooperate more closely. I'll say more about the deployment of materials in Section 6 later on.

Suffice it to say at this point that in planning the ethnological part of Section 8—the main part of the hall—I had decided to go with what was clearly the strength of our collections and to devote my half of Section 8 to the native cultures of Amazonia. Thus the Chaco, Pampas-Patagonia, and Tierra del Fuego would get short shrift, being fitted into my part of Section 6, which was no more than half the space.

Accordingly, going with our strength, Laila and I were to spend months painstakingly picking through the four storerooms for ethnographic objects from Amazonia.

The artifacts which, week after week, we selected from these store rooms we took down to the floor below where they were housed temporarily in a large room which had previously served as a staging area for the objects that eventually went into the Asia hall. Here, behind the doors of old glass-fronted storage cabinets the specimens rested until our new Hahn cases were ready to receive them.

When that day would come depended on a number of factors. First of all, we had to determine just where each exhibit case was to be positioned on the floor. Then the inside of each case had to be made safe to hold the artifacts, some of them rather delicate. That story will be told a little later.

*   *   *   *

In the year and a half that we spent selecting candidates for exhibition, Laila and I handled just about all the 15,000 or so artifacts in the four Amazonian store rooms, ending up with something under 1,000 candidates. The work, tedious though it was, turned out to be more than just routine. While most of the artifacts were familiar to us, every now and then we came across an item we could not readily identify and were forced to turn to the catalog volumes which we always kept by our side for just those situations.

Our aim while going through this procedure, was to bring Amazonian Indian culture to life in its rich variety and to do by selecting material from as many different tribes as possible.

It was tedious work, as I indicated, and Laila and I—we always worked together on this—usually limited our time in the store rooms to no more than an hour and a half a day. Longer than this, we found our circuits becoming overloaded and the work growing wearisome instead of enjoyable.

The conditions we worked under were anything but ideal. The store rooms were not climate controlled. It would be an exaggeration to say that we shivered in winter and sweated in summer, but late spring and early fall were the times we could say we were comfortable. Moreover since there was no ventilation in the store rooms they were always stuffy. And since many of the artifacts were on open shelves instead of inside drawers, the dust of decades had settled over them.

There was only one light in each of the store rooms, situated just above the door leading into them. Thus, when we needed to penetrate deep into the store rooms we had to carry a portable work light attached to a long extension cord plugged into a socket near the door.

One small redeeming feature of this work was that whenever we opened the door to the Montaña store room we were greeted with the wonderful scent of vanilla which, even after decades of captivity in that room, refused to be dispelled.

Though we worked under less than optimal conditions, we were spurred on by the thought that after this grinding routine was over we could look forward to the rewarding part of exhibit work: the actual installing of the chosen artifacts in their designated exhibit cases t and watch the story they were to tell begin to unfold.

*   *   *   *

I have been unsparing in describing the hardships we underwent in the store rooms because all that is now a thing of the past. Today, thanks largely to the vision, energy, and skill of Paul Beelitz, our collections manager, the anthropology collections of the American Museum are stored under world class conditions. Indeed museum curators come from all over to cast an admiring eye—perhaps even an envious one—on the way our artifacts are housed and cared for, taking careful notes as they go. And Paul is always pleased and proud to answer their questions and explain how the remarkable transformation was achieved.

*   *   *   *

But now back to the South American hall.

The specimens we brought down from the sixth-floo store rooms were first given a light cleaning, and if they needed some form of repair they were turned over to our conservators for the appropriate treatment. The rest of the them, as I said, were placed in large cabinets in the staging room, there to await installation in the Hahn cases. Once these cases, of which there were several dozen, had been positioned in their ultimate locations, they pretty well filled the hall, but leaving ample space for visitors to maneuver their way around them.

As soon as the workmen performing the herculean task of flooring over the well in the floor above us, work could proceed on the next phase of the operation, namely, the installation of the exhibit cases in their designated locations. Laila and I, in consultation with Gene Bergmann, had already pretty well decided just where the cases were to go. Their distribution on the floor, as they snaked their way inside the hall, was carefully thought out, being calculated to maximize the surface area of glass through which the objects inside them could be viewed.

The physical labor of actually placing the cases was carried out with great precision. Care was taken with every aspect of this work. After all, the installers were handling three-quarters of a million dollars' worth of finely machined glass and steel.

With rare exceptions, the individual Hahn cases were not free standing. They were grouped one against another and thus had to be fitted together with exactitude. Every measurement preceding their placement was made with an accuracy virtually down to the millimeter, since the cases had to dovetail precisely.

As you might imagine, not just anyone could have installed those cases. Certainly not the artists in our Exhibition department. The Hahn Company, jealous of the high standards they strove to maintain, had in fact made a special arrangement with an engineering firm in Baltimore to install their cases in whatever museum had purchased them.

During the time the cases were being fitted into their places Laila and I watched in admiration but stayed out of the way. Our turn would come.

The cases were state-of-the-art when it came to displaying exhibit specimen. Their one drawback had to do with their size.

Displaying outsize objects was a problem. The dimensions of the space inside the standard Hahn case was approximately 5 feet by 5 feet by 3 feet. This made it difficult to exhibit tall artifacts the way we would have wished. This was especially true of blowguns, which are often 8 to 10 feet long. Since a blowgun hunter, when pointing his weapon at a monkey in the treetops, holds his blowgun almost straight up, we would have liked to do the same with our manikin. But that was out of the question. To deal with this problem as best we could we ended up having to remove the bottom of the blowgun exhibit case to give us a little more height. For structural reasons it was not possible to remove the top. We also resorted to using the shortest blowgun we had and pairing it with a short blowgun hunter. Even so we were forced to have the hunter point his weapon at well under the 180 degrees we would have liked.

Here is an important lesson a curator soon has to learn. Exhibit work entails a series of compromises, with complete realism being rarely achievable.

Another constraint in ethnological exhibit work is the following: while it is always best to show an artifact in use, much of the time the curator has to show it simply lying inertly on the floor of the case or affixed flat against the case wall. One way to introduce some semblance of realism into an exhibit is to show the artifact in the hands or around the neck or waist of a manikin. In this regard, we found manikins to be a great adjunct to our exhibit, as will be described.

We also liked to display materials that are ancillary to the artifact which is the primary focus of the scene being portrayed.

The blowgun provides a prime example of this.

The reason the blowgun is such an effective hunting weapon is that its darts are tipped with the famous poison, curare, which soon renders an animal immobile, and not long after brings about its death. Therefor in any blowgun exhibit curare must play a significant role. And it does so in ours.

A shallow dish of curare—the real thing—sits next to an assortment of blowgun darts, the tips of which were smeared with it before the hunter inserted them into the barrel of his blowgun.

I am no stranger to curare. As a matter of fact at one time there was enough of it in my office to kill ten thousand monkeys!

Here is the story behind that remarkable assertion.

Curare as found in a museum's store room is not a single substance. In the form it isapplied to blowgun darts curare usually consists of a dozen or more ingredients. All but one of them, however, have what we would regard as a "magical" effect on an animal shot with it. As best we can tell only one ingredient has an actual physiological effect on its victim. This active element is the sap of the vine *Strychnos toxifera*. This sap contains a muscle relaxant which science has found to be so effective medically that it is used in such procedures as delicate eye surgery and for easing the pain of a difficult childbirth. As a result of this useful property curare began to be imported into this country, primarily from Ecuador.

But then, as so often happens, curare began to be synthesized in the laboratory, eventually becoming cheaper when produced in this way than when imported.

This meant that the curare in possession of importers could no longer be sold at a profit. Consequently a major curare importer found itself with a large supply of it on hand and no market for it.

Not knowing how to dispose of it and being afraid to simply throw it away, the importer turned over its supply to the Museum, figuring that we would know just how to dispose of it.

But before someone in the Museum found what to do with it (this was before my time) it was kept under what ultimately became my desk.

Most of it was eventually gotten rid of in some way (probably by simply flushing it down the toilet) but a limited quantity was held on to—anticipating, perhaps, that some day it might be draw on for a blowgun exhibit in some future South American hall.

*   *   *   *

I have mentioned the shortcomings of the Hahn cases for displaying long artifacts. I need now to mentioning their great advanges, which far outweigh their disadvantages. Of these the primary one is their accessibility. Formerly, with our old exhibit cases, whenever we needed to enter a case to dust the insides or adjust an artifact that had shifted, we had to wait for four carpenters to be ready with their huge suction cups to remove the heavy glass front of a case and then replace it. Now, with the Hahn cases, entering the case could be done by one person by simply sliding the glass font onto a track and pushing it along with as little as one finger.

There was however, that there was another difficulty with the Hahn cases. But his one was not peculiar to the Hahn cases alone but was shared with other types of cases as well. When two cases are to be fitted together at right angles to each other, edge to edge, a mullion is created thereby, impeding the visitor's view of what ia behind it in the case.

Here, though, Gene Bergmann's ingenuity came to the rescue. His simple and elegant solution was to eliminate the mullion altogether by designing a new and larger form of case, triangular in shape with its apex pointing backward and a broad glass front. This type of case provided the visitor with an unimpeded view of the entire conents of it.

This new design also provided considerably more space for exhibits than the standard Hahn case. I'll return to the importance of this in a moment.

So simple and effective was this new design that it must have surprised the Hahn company that they had not come up with it themselves. At any rate, they liked it so well that, in addition to making a number of them for our use they incorporated the design into their standard line of cases.

We took advantage of Gene's design to improve the way we could present certain of our exhibits.

First, though, let me introduce manioc, the highest yielding crop plant in the world, and the staple food of most Amazonian tribes. Besides its great yield manioc has other qualities that have made it the principal cultivated plant of virtually every tribe in the Amazon. It is extremely draught resistant, surviving easily the two or more rainless months experienced by various regions of Amazonia. Moreover, manioc has no fixed harvest time so It can be allowed to stay in the ground until needed.

(However, it cannot be left in the ground indefinitely since after six months or so, when the tuber reaches its greatest size and maximum starch conent, it becomes woody and difficult to deal with.)

The one serious drawback to manioc is that many varieties of it contain lethal amounts of cyanide in the form of prussic acid. Needless to say, this must be removed from the tuber before it can be rendered edible.

Of the various processes Amazonian Indians make use of in their daily lives none is more important than the one used to remove the deadly prussic acid from the tuber. This process has long been of particular interest to me and I was determined to show at least the major phases of it in the hall. However, the process is complex, having several variants, each with a series of steps.

The most sophisticated of these is the one which culminates in the use of the celebrated manioc press called the *tipiti*. I won't try to describe this device here except to say that it is so ingenuous that it led the great English anthropologist E. B. Tylor to speak of it in glowing terms.

We have a number of *tipitís* in our collections and one of them, along with an explanation of just how it works, is the centerpiece of the manioc exhibit.

But to show even some of the steps in the various methods of manioc processing required a good deal of space—more than afforded by the standard Hahn case. It fitted in nicely, however, in the extra space provided by Gene's new exhibit case.

*   *   *   *

Before leaving agriculture and the use we made of the triangular cases, I will say a thing or two about the second most important crop plant of Amazonia—maize—and how we presented the Indians' use of it in the exhibit.

Although it plays second fiddle to manioc among most tribes, a few of them located in western Amazonia, raise more of it than they do of manioc. Moreover, we had enough items related to corn in the store rooms to do a creditable job of it. We had, for example, some ears of corn with multi-colored kernels that I'd brought back from the Amahuaca. In fact the Amahuaca grow so much maize that the average family harvests 25,000 to 30,000 ears a year— enough so that some families build a special corn crib to store it all. One photograph in the exhibit shows unhusked earpiled neatly, row upon row, in a crib.

Every few days a woman goes to the corn crib and picks out a few dozen ears to bring back to her house, where she shells them, puts the loose kernels in a pot, and toasts them over a fire. The kernels are then ground into a fine powder in a wooden mortar and pestle. This cornmeal, called *mïto,* may be eaten, a pinch at a time, and is delicious. However, it is so dry that one's mouth soon grinds to a halt. More commonly, *mïto* is mixed with water and boiled into a gruel.

Among the Kuikuru, a thousand miles to the east, maize is also grown but on a more limited scale. Although all forty men in the village have one or more manioc gardens, only four of them had cornfields. At harvest time they brought their entire corn crop back to the village where it was laid out in the plaza for everyone to share A sort of first fruits ceremony occurs at this time during which the boys are whipped with a cotton waist band, "to make them grow tall."

* * * *

Once more let me return to the triangular cases and indicate how they helped with our oversize exhibits. They enabled us to display comfortably several exhibits which otherwise would have had to be crammed into a space too small for them, if they could have been exhibited at all.

For example, one such exhibit was a miniature representation of the Kuikuru village as it looked when I was last there in 1975. In making this diorama we had to foreshorten the scene somewhat in order to show at least a few manioc gardens surrounding the village. Except for this, everything else in this diorama is in proper scale.

Much of the area around the Kuikuru village is forested, and to represent the trees we used Norway moss which makes a neat stand-in for tiny trees. This was an exhibition trick made known to us by Ray de Lucia, one of the preparators in the Exhibition department. This is but one instance of how much we relied on the vast experience of the preparators in putting together our hall.

Another way in which we utilized the extra space provided by Gene's triangular case involved the exhibit of a Canpa (Ashaninka) woman, stretched out and weaving a *cushma* (a long night-shirt-like garment) on a backstrap loom. This was the only full-size manikin we were able to salvage from the old South American hall and incorporate into the new hall. All the other manikins we used were created especially for the new hall.

Finally, to cite just one more exhibit enhanced by, if not requiring, the triangular case, I would point to that of *kuarup,* which has become the most famous Amazonian ceremony and about which I will have more to say. This ceremony, whose center of attention consists of several massive memorial posts—three of which we have represented in the hall—called for ample space if it was going to look authentic. The triangular case made this possible.

Altogether the Hahn cases, standard or augmented, proved not only serviceable but a distinct asset as regards the appearance of the hall, being undeniably handsome.

This elegance, of course, comes at a price. In fact, as already stated, their total cost was in the neighborhood of three-quarters of a million dollars.

There was, however, a way in which this cost could be slightly reduced. Not all the Hahn cases, once in place, would be free standing. Many of them would be positioned with their backs against the masonry walls of the building. Therefor they would not require expensive glass panels on all four sides. The side abutting the wall, though, would have to have some kind of backing other than just the bare wall. The obvious choice for this backing was plywood, which was much cheaper than the original, precision-cut glass panels of the Hahn cases.

Plywood, however, has a serious disadvantage which had to be dealt with. The adhesive substance used to bond the several layers of plywood to each other gives off urea formaldehyde fumes—which, we learned from our conservator, would be harmful to the more sensitive objects, especially the pre-Columbian textiles.

To overcome this problem the plywood had to be clad in some way. One way was to cover it over with a thin film of aluminum. We looked into this and found that doing so for all the cases that would require it would cost about a hundred thousand dollars.

Knowing that the director had already laid out close to a million dollars for the

Hahn cases themselves, we were reluctant to approach him with a request for even more money. No, some other, cheaper colution had to be found to the formaldehyde problem.

After much research, our conservator, Nancy Demyttenaere (the first objects conservator the Anthropology department had ever hired) told us that Dupont made a paint called Korlar which, if applied in three coats, each one running in a different direction, and if together they built up a thickness of three mills (three one-thousandths of an inch) this would form a barrier that would keep the formaldehyde fumes at bay.

So this is what we did. And I can report that after more than thirty years the technique has proved successful.

*   *   *   *

I should say that in planning the Amazonian section of the hall I had made it a point to visit the corresponding exhibits of both the Field Museum in Chicago and the Smithsonian in Washington, D.C. I was determined to make our hall at least as good as theirs—and, frankly, to surpass them. Nor did I think after visiting our sister institutions that this would prove to be impossible. And, when all is said and done, I am satisfied that we achieved the objective.

Since, as I have explained, the focus of our part of the hall would be on the strength of our collections— Amazonia—the Chaco, the Pampas and Patagonia, as well as Tierra del Fuego would be playing second fiddle. There simply wasn't enough space to exhibit them all adequately. Moreover (with the possible exception of the Chaco) our collections were not deepenough for these areas to be able to do so.

Having made this decision, the question still remained as to how best to exhibit the culture of Amazonia. Once the starring role had been awarded to this area, I still had to decide Just how this rich culture could best be portrayed. Basically there were two ways of doing so. Amazonia could be divided into its various cultural sub-areas, each one being assigned a portion of the 4,000 square feet of space available to us. Alternatively I could deal with Amazonia as a whole, with its culture being divided topically instead of regionally. It could be divided into the major cultural categories—subsistence, social structure, and religion—and then subdivided into various sub-categories.

The choice turned out to be easy. To begin with, there were several reasons against dividing Amazonia into regional sub-areas.

While the overall coverage of Amazonia in our store rooms was good, our coverage of the individual sub-areas was uneven. Some were covered distinctly better than others. Thus we could not have done equal justice to each sub-area and the disparity between them would have been evident.

Moreover, enough cultural similarity exists between the various sub-areas to have made for considerable overlap between them, and for the duplication to have been noticeable.

So our course was clear. Vast as it was, we would tackle Amazonia as a unit, dealing with the various cultural categories in order, in much the same way as is done in a standard ethnographic monograph. We would begin with such categories as settlement pattern and house type, proceed to subsistence ... and end with mythology and the afterworld.

Nevertheless the question still remained as to how to proceed within each of these cultural categories. After some reflection on the matter the concept that seemed to make the most sense was that of *theme* and *variation*.

For example, under the theme of hunting, the various sub-themes—the variations— would be hunting with bow and arrow, hunting with the blowgun, hunting with traps, and so forth.

I thought we needed to make the idea of theme and variation more tangible by providing visitors with a concrete example of the organizing concept of the hall as soon as they stepped into the introductory alcove.

*   *   *   *

Before proceeding any further along this line I should pause, take a few steps backward, and say something of the overall layout of the entire South American hall.

Visitors enter it from the Mesoamerican archaeology hall, pass through a mixed part of the hall (Section 6) in which they would find archaeology and ethnology interspersed. Passing through this section they would turn right and enter what Craig and I both considered to be the *real* South American hall—to which we each devoted the major part of our efforts.

This main section (Section 8 of the Museum), which lies on the west side of the building, has a total area of 8,000 square feet. Craig and I divided this area equally between us: one half of it to archaeology and the other half to ethnology (although we usually speak of them loosely as *ethnography* halls.)

Craig and I had never discussed who would get the northern half of this space

(Section 8) and who would get the southern half. I had not revealed my preference to him, nor had he revealed his preference to me. Hence, since I assumed our preferences would coincide, I thought we might have to arm wrestle to decide the issue.

But it never came to that. As it turned out, all along Craig had wanted the southern half of Section 8 whereas I wanted the northern half. Thus the anticipated arm wrestling never materialized.

The northern half—the end I wanted—was something of a cul- de sac—which was precisely why I preferred it. I did not want my section of the hall to be a passageway leading to other exhibits, toward which visitors would be heading without necessarily paying much attention to mine.

And, being a cul-de-sac, if visitors wandered into it inadvertently and felt like a captive audience, I wanted them to conclude, after a few minutes' stay, that their "captivity" was worth the error.

With regard to our choice of sections, I had no idea whether Craig had thought of the question the way I did. Obviously not, or he would have made a different choice. But I never knew, since we never discussed the matter.

After having divided the 8,00 square feet of Section 8 to our mutual satisfaction, Craig went on to divide his 4,000 square feet even further. At the suggestion of Gene Bergmann, half of Craig's section was kept at floor level while the other half—the half abutting my section—was raised some four feet above floor level, creating a sort of platform. By so doing, Craig ended up with two different levels of exhibits, the lower one he devoted to the coastal cultures of prehistoric Peru, such as Mochica and

Chimú, and the upper one devoted to the highland cultures, such as Wari and the Inca—or Inka, as he preferred to spell it, which has become standard practice among Peruvian archaeologists.

A ramp led from the coastal cultures on floor level up to the highland cultures on the platform. Then from the north end of the platform another ramp led down into the Amazon.

Walking down this ramp visitors would see on the wall, flanking the ramp on their left, two large photographs. The first was of an Inca fortress, betokening the highland cultures the visitors were about to leave, and the second photograph showing a tangle of meandering rivers wending their way through the rainforest, suggesting to visitors the kind of environment which was home to the Indians whose culture they were about to encounter.

* * * *

Here, though, I foresaw a problem. As they stood there, poised at the top of the ramp, considering whether or not to make the descent, visitors would already have walked a fair piece in the Museum; very likely they were tired; their feet might be hurting; they would in all likelihood be hungry; they needed to go to the bathroom. How, then, could I l induce them to proceed down the ramp and into my domain?

I had to make whatever they saw straight ahead of them as they looked down the ramp, inviting enough to make them forget their complaints and take those last few steps into Amazonia.

Once they did so, I was confident we could hold them—indeed, entice them to continue, willingly enough, the rest of the way into the cultural realm that lay ahead of them.

Again, how was I to get them to take those last few steps down the ramp? Actually, long before, I had in my mind confronted the problem, and had decided what I would dot. I would place, front and center, at the foot of the ramp our most spectacular ceremonial costume. I was familiar enough with our Amazonian collections to know just which costume that would be. It was that of a Wayana man with long flowing strips of bark hanging from a headdress which bristled with long, red macaw tail feathers.

Attractive as it was, this costume would be mainly "for show," meant to draw the visitors in. Besides appealing to their eyes I wanted to engage their minds. And one way to do so, as I already explained, was to introduce them to the concept that would guide them through the rest of the hall—namely, *theme and variation.* Carried out throughout the exhibits, I hoped this conceptual device would plant in their minds the logic governing the layout of the exhibits.

In the end, I wanted visitors to feel that what they had witnessed as they strolled through the hall was more than just an interesting assortment of artifacts. I wanted them to think of them as forming part of an integrated ensemble representing the ways in which the Indians of Amazonia had successfully adapted themselves to their rainforest environment.

As I indicated above, to make the idea of theme and variation more tangible I would apply it to a particular kind of artifact—the *composite comb.*

Throughout most of the primitive world—especially in Africa and Melanesia—combs are made by cutting teeth into a single piece of wood or other material. In Amazonia, though, combs are made by cutting each tooth individually and then binding the teeth together in some way. Combs made in this fashion are known as *composite combs*. So the *theme* here was that of combs in general; the *variation* came in the variety of ways in which they are joined together. It is in this way that one tribe's combs can be distinguished from those of another. The combs of the Karajá, for instance, are immediately distinguishable from those of the Kuikuru. The teeth of the former are coarse, those of the latter are slender.

The very first exhibit unit we finished and installed in the hall consisted of a map of Amazonia on which a dozen or so composite combs had been placed, each positioned over the spot on the map where the tribe that made that comb resided.

In order to show that composite combs formed a distinct class of artifacts, different from other forms of comb, high on this map we placed a comb made by the Djuka (Bush Negroes) of Suriname which is quite different from any made by an Amazonian group.

*   *   *   *

On a second map, adjacent to the first, we leave theme and variation behind and turn to locating every tribe represented in the hall by at least one artifact. In that way a visitor, wanting to know where a certain tribe was located, could easily determine it with a glance at the map.

I have made no actual count of the number of tribes on this map but it must be in the neighborhood of a hundred.

I use the word "tribe" here very loosely to refer to any identifiable native group, which is the way the word is generally used by anthropologists when they have no more specific designation for a group. There is no better word in common use that carries the same umbrella of meaning. It is a vague term, to be sure, but nevertheless a useful one. We need a commonly understood term to distinguish one native group from another and "tribe" is as good as any. Hence I will continue it use it in this broad sense.

Now, if one is used to thinking of a tribe in a more restricted sense as a society (like that of the Cheyenne) as not only being a distinct grouping of people with a common language and culture, which aggregates seasonally into a multi-community political unit, then tribes do not exist in Amazonia.

Basically the socio-political structure in this part of the world was, and continues to be, one of autonomous villages.

Some may be familiar with the loose association of villages found in the Upper Xingú and wonder what to call it. Is it an exception to the rule? Actually it is more of a socio-ceremonial entity than a political one.

However, here and there in Amazonia, under special conditions beyond the scope of this book to go into, multi-village polities—*chiefdoms*—were formed. But these were rare. Again, it is worth emphasizing that Village autonomy is the rule in Amazonia.

*   *   *   *

By means of color coding, on the map just alluded to we show the distribution of the major language families of Amazonia.

According to Čestmir Loukotka, a leading South American linguist, there are close to a hundred language families in Amazonia. Not languages, mind you, but language *families*. This is a bewildering number indicating extraordinary linguistic diversity. However, on our map we show only the ten most important families. In a few cases, like that of the Trumai of the Upper Xingú, a language family may be represented by only a single village. In the large majority of cases, though, a language family has dozens of tribes representing it.

* * * *

Even before Laila made it a point to stressed its importance, I was aware of the utility of photographs as a way to enhance the appearance of the hall, to say nothing of imparting information about its exhibits. Moreover, by portraying human beings in action with artifacts in their hands they would inject life into the objects otherwise lying inert bn the floor of an exhibit case. The gathering baskets, digging sticks and fire fans behind the glass panels could then be seen as instruments which human beings used in their everyday interaction with nature.

We also felt that visitors would like to see Amazonian Indians, not only as wielders of implements, but as flesh and blood individuals. Thus In the introductory alcove into which the visitors were now descending, photograph would give them their first glimpse of the Indians whose culture they were about to encounter. They would show their physical appearance as well as their distinctive tribal decorations: their manner of dress (or undress), their facial features, lip plugs, ear ornaments, and so on.

Originally I had assumed that we would put up black-and-white photographs of moderate size, but Laila soon convinced me that the exhibit would be much more effective if the photos were of large size and in full color. And how right she was!

How could we not take full advantage, for example, of the vibrant red of *urucú,* which is such a prominent element in the Indians' manner of decoration? Not only do they apply it freely to their faces and bodies, they often color their artifacts with it.

However, I must say that in this sea of scarlet the most distinctive face among a dozen photographs is not in red at all. It belongs to Yarima, a young Yanomamö woman, resplendent in white bird down which has been carefully applied to her hair.

About Yarima there is much to say. First let me say that few museum curators of an ethnographic exhibit have had the experience of having a native he has known in the field, some years later be brought to his museum and there come face to face with an image of herself taken years earlier when she was in her village.

Or, similarly, has an Amazonian Indian seen, mounted behind glass, an artifact fashioned by his own hands that he had traded to the curator for a pair of scissors?

I have had this experience. Twice.

The first time was when Afukaká, the chief of the Kuikuru village I lived in, saw, affixed to the wall next to others like it, the comb he had made for me some twenty years before. Afukaká had been brought to New York by Sandra Wellington, director of the Indian Museum in Brasília and a great friend and benefactor of the Indians of the Upper Xingú.

I first met Afukaká in 1953 when he was a three-year-old boy whose name was then Uisapá. Only years later did he inherit the name of his grandfather, the illustrious Afukaká, well remembered in the village as having been a great chief. The Kuikuru often referred to Uisapá in my presence as "capitáo kúsagï" (little chief), giving me to know that in time he would succeed to his grandfather's office.

When I met him again in 1975, twenty-two years later, Afukaká had already become chief of the village. He was well liked but whether he would ever command the great respect his grandfather had enjoyed, only time would tell.

Indeed when I was with him in 1975 the degree of obedience given to his directions was still somewhat like that accorded to the typical Tropical Forest village headman, which has been humorously characterized by one ethnologist familiar with Amazonia in the epigram: "One word from the chief, and everyone does as he pleases."

And as a matter of fact, I once witnessed an example of just this response to Afukaká's commands.

One day when I was living with the Kuikuru I wanted to see a fish poisoning expedition and mentioned this to Afukaká who said he would organize one for me. Accordingly he called out to the men around him to go into the forest and cut some *timbó* (fish poisoning vines) for me. The only ones who stirred were some teenage boys, who were always ready for any sort of adventure. The men stayed where they were, not wishing to appear to hop to it at anyone's behest but their own.

Eventually, though, a few men ambled off to fetch some *timbó*, but only as if it were their own idea, not that of the chief's.

I understand though that by the time he visited New York in the 1990s, Afukaká had attained a good deal more of the respect and authority that had been accorded his grandfather.

Besides the comb, now resting behind glass in the Museum, Afukaká made one other item for me, this one meant for me personally, not to be turned over to the Museum. It was a finger ring he carved from a black palm nut. It felt a trifle loose on my finger but I wore it anyway. Then one night, several years later, while I was dancing a spirited polka on the shores of Lake Tahoe, a vigorous arm gesture caused the ring to fly off my finger. The dance floor was covered with a dark carpet against which the ring did not stand out, and search as we did for it the ring was never found.

* * * *

The other instance of someone I had known in the field having come to New York and seen herself pictured in the South

American hall was the aforementioned Yarima, who had the unique distinction of having married her anthropologist. I first met Yarima in the Yanomamö village of Hasubuwateri when she was a girl of about nine., By way of a preface let me say that during my three stints of ethnographic field work in Amazonia I have discovered a sure-fire way to establish rapport with the natives. It worked like a charm with the Kuikuru, it worked just as well with the Amahuaca, and again with the Yanomamö. People in all three villages—especially the younger ones—enjoyed "Old McDonald Had a Farm" immensely, my full-throated rendition of "a chick-chick here," "a quack-quack there," "everywhere an oink-oink," and all the other animal sounds seemed to delight them.

When I sang it to a group of young women and girls in Hasubuwateri I found I had a most appreciative audience. So much so that they weren't satisfied with just three choruses of "Old McDonald." When I told them that would be enough, they refused to believe me, insisting on more. And when I still demurred, four or five of them jumped on me and pinned me to the ground until I agreed to sing it again … and again … and again.

I can't swear to it but I think Yarima was one of the girls who pinned me down, but I like to think it was.

Years later, when she stood in front of her likeness in the Museum, Yarima was no longer a bouncy young girl, but a sedate married woman, with probably little recollection of that incident. I, however, will never forget it.

Yarima didn't linger long over her photograph in the exhibit but, accompanied by her husband, Ken Good, moved on to the Museum cafeteria, there to enjoy the one item of Western cuisine she really liked—French fried potatoes.

*   *   *   *

All of this, though, is getting a little ahead of the story. Let me go back to the time I started working at the Museum, in September, 1957, as Assistant Curator of South American Ethnology. The first question I can recall being asked in those early days had to do with shrunken heads, probably the best known item in our ethnological collections. And questions on this topic never seemed to end. The public's fascination with these trophy heads appears to be endless. Moreover, it soon became evident that it must also have been among the questions most often asked of my predecessor, Harry Tschopik, for in my first days on the job I found in one of his desk drawers an index card with the name and address of a certain Ben Rosenberg, a dealer on 43rd Street who had a most unusual double specialty: second-hand microscopes and shrunken heads. The index card also informed me that the going price for a genuine shrunken head in those days was $200. But just as with everything else, Inflation has impacted the shrunken head market. Not long ago I received a phone call from a milling executive in Minneapolis who had been offered a shrunken head— said to be genuine—for $20,000.

It should not be surprising that the American Museum should have received so many inquiries about shrunken heads since over the years the word has gotten around that we have one of the world's premier collections of them.

Already, when I started working at the Museum, there was a good deal of lore to be heard about how we had acquired our shrunken heads. One piece of lore which I'm sure contained at least a modicum of truth to it is the following:

During a trip to Ecuador a man bought a shrunken head (probably in Guayaquil) and brought it home. From the outset his wife hated the thing and made him keep it in the closet. But when the man died, his widow's first act, after a decent period of mourning, was to wrap up the head, being careful to handle it as little as possible, and donated it to the Museum, feeling herself well rid of the thing.

Be that as it may, I sometimes wish I had recorded all the stories about shrunken heads that have come to my ears over the years. I'll recount just one of them, my favorite, which I can vouch for since I was involved.

One day I got a phone call from a young woman who wanted to know everything about the appearance of shrunken heads. Were the ears pierced? Were the eyebrows shaved off? Were the lips stitched together? Was the hair long? And so on.

Finally, curious to learn why she wanted to know about shrunken heads in such exhaustive detail, I asked her if she would mind telling me.

"Not at all," she replied, and proceeded to explain to me with the greatest *sangue froid:* "You see, I'm a fifth grade school teacher in Yonkers, and this year our class project is to make *papier maché* shrunken heads, and I wanted to be sure the students got every detail just right."

Well, I too wanted to get every detail just right so that whenever I was asked about head shrinking could reply authoritatively. Accordingly, early in the game, I turned to Michael Harner's *The Jívaro,* which still ranks as the "Bible" when it comes to such matters. Harner was an anthropologist who carried out extensive field work in Amazonia, especially among the head-shrinking Jívaro. (They are more properly referred to as the Shuar, but since they are so well known by the name Jívaro that I will continue to call them that.)

While he was with them, Harner made a careful study of head shrinking. It's all there in his book, and had I been thinking ahead in those days to the South American hall, I would surely have made a mental note to consult *The Jívaro* when the time came to begin working on it. And in fact, when the time did come and we needed material to write label copy for the shrunken head case, it was Harner's book that we turned to. But more about that shortly.

In the meantime I had learned all I needed to know about the subject to answer any casual inquiries about it.

With this much as a background let me jump ahead a bit to the stage in the installation of head shrinking when we had to put our knowledge of the subject into words.

From the start we knew we had to be particularly careful in preparing the label copy for this exhibit. We certainly did not want to sensationalize the practice since we didn't want to portray it as an example of "ye savage customs of ye heathen."

Instead we intended to make head shrinking, while unique in the primitive world, nevertheless understood as reasonable and intelligible, given the complex set of Jívaro beliefs about war raids and the desire for revenge.

* * * *

Since the matter of label copy has come to the fore, it is a good time to discuss this important aspect of exhibit work.

Perhaps because I am very near sighted I have always disliked long labels, which require a good deal. This is particularly so because long labels are usually set in small type. In fact I am disinclined even to begin reading such labels.

But at the same time, I feel that a natural history museum (unlike an art museum) is obligated to impart to the visitor a substantial amount of information about the object or the subject shown in front of him.

So that is the Cilla and Charybdis that a curator has to navigate between when writing the label for a display. On the one hand, he doesn't want to shortchange his viewers, but then neither does he want to overwhelm them with details.

Laila and I took writing label copy very seriously. Either one of us would write the first draft and then show it to the other. In this way the label copy went back and forth between us until we felt we could not improve it any further.

That however was not the end of the story. The Exhibition department had a professional label copy editor, Peggy Cooper, to whom we would send each label when we had exhausted our ability to make it any better. Peggy read it over with her critical eye and made her suggestions, if she could, for improving it. Almost always we found her suggestions reasonable and accepted them.

And so every label in the hall has undergone a thorough vetting.

* * * *

Without a doubt the Jívaro shrunken heads were a major focus of the hall. But by no means did we want it to overshadow the rest of the exhibits. After all, it was only one case among many, and the smallest cases at that. Let me then continue with the installation.

Standard ethnographic monographs attempt to co cover all aspects of the culture of the society they are dealing with—or at least the major ones. Our aim was to do the same.

One of the longest stretches of a society's activities has to do with the life cycle. After all, it begins with the birth of a person and ends with his death. Not every ethnographic exhibit hall in a museum attempts to present the various stages of the life cycle. It is not easy to do because, for one thing, it is not always possible to find the artifacts necessary to illustrate each major phase of the sequence. However, we thought our store rooms were rich enough to provide the material required to carry it off. Furthermore we felt we had sufficient imagination to fill in those parts of the sequence that required evocative descriptions rather than artifacts.

Our life cycle section begins with a poignant photograph showing a mother and her infant child sitting on the ground and looking soulfully into each other's eyes. The photographer had the good luck of capturing the two at precisely the right moment to produce a memorable image Skipping ahead beyond a photograph showing what fun Indian boys are capable of, we illustrated young girlhood through the doll making proclivities of Pacho, an Amahuaca girl. Pacho, who was about twelve-year-old, can hardly be considered typical of Amazonian girls, for at that tender age she had already been married five times. Although her four previous marriages had ended in failure, her fifth one, despite the age difference between her and her husband, seemed to be a very happy one. One of the pleasant memories I have of my time with the Amahuaca is of seeing Pacho trying to drape her little arm affectionately around the shoulders of her 37-year-old husband, Hawachiwayamba, as they sat together on a log bench.

But the reason I bring Pacho into the picture at this point is that one of her dolls is on display in this exhibit.

Pacho loved to make dolls, and the notable thing about them is that already at the age of twelve she had developed her own distinctive style. There was no mistaking whose doll that was. Her dolls were identifiable as hers, just as much as a van Gogh painting is easily identifiable as his.

The most striking feature of Pacho's dolls was that their cheeks always came to a point. Moreover, she never considered a doll finished until she had snipped off a few strands of her hair and plastered them onto the doll's head, securing them in place with a lump of wet clay.

By way of contrast, Pacho's older sister, Yúyupa, had her own distinctive style of doll making, quite unlike that of her sister. Thus we can see that even at a tender age individuality will assert itself.

*   *   *   *

One of the many contributions Laila made to the hall, as I have already indicated, was in stressing the value of photographs in bringing exhibits to life. As a result, the South American hall is peppered with photos. A good example of this is the large size of an Indian house which can be fixed in the mind with a striking photograph in a way words alone could not begin to convey.

Take the word *maloca,* which has come to mean any sort of Indian house, but which originally was restricted to a large Indian house containing within its wall the entire village. The Witoto *maloca* shown by a photo in the settlement section of the hall, is so large that, as the saying goes, it makes the people standing around it look like ants.

Photos are especially good at capturing emotions. This is particularly apparent in the case of puberty rituals, which often have the character of ordeals. Here photographs leave no doubt about the pain that initiate may suffer.

A notable example of a harsh puberty rite is the ant ordeal of the Guianas. A photograph in this section shows this unmistakably. An Indian boy who is about to undergo this ordeal is having clapped to his chest a straw plaque into which a hundred stinging ants have been woven. As the ants struggle to free themselves, they sting anything they come in contact with. The face of the unfortunate boy shows full well that he knows what is in store for him.

This puberty ritual is indeed a severe one. However among the tribes of the Upper Xingú the puberty rite undergone by pubescent girls is much milder. It involves little more discomfort for her than being placed in seclusion behind a screened-off area of her house. She is not allowed to engage in strenuous physical activities. Nor is she permitted to leave the house except at night. Also, for the full year of her seclusion she is not supposed to cut her bangs. When at last she emerges from seclusion she is at her most marriageable, and should she marry then, part of the ceremony consists of the groom cutting her bangs. As the photograph in the exhibit shows, these have grown long enough to cover her eyes.

By way of contrast the puberty ritual which Kuikuru boys undergo is much more rigorous. Besides being secluded for a year—as a girl is—the boy goes with his father to a swampy area where they search until they find an anaconda. The boy is then supposed to wrestle the snake, allowing himself to be bitten on the forearm. He then kills the snake, cuts off its tail, and skins it. Later he carves the replica of an anaconda tail out of some light wood and covers it with the snake's own skin. This adornment, which is emblematic of his hardihood, he wears dangling down his back during certain ceremonies.

While I was doing field work among the Kuikuru in 1953-54 I knew a boy— actually, a young man—by the name of

Uluti who was undergoing a delayed puberty initiation. His father having died, an uncle was supervising his initiation. But Uluti, who was older than most initiates, was difficult to control and broke seclusion several times.

At the age of about seventeen Uluti was already a massive physical specimen. It seemed to me that when he grew to full manhood he would become wrestling champion of the Upper Xingú—a great distinction which brings distinction throughout a man's life. By the time I returned to the Kuikuru village twenty-two years later, sure enough, my prediction had come true. Although by then retired from the sport, Uluti had indeed become wrestling champion of the Upper Xingú, and his fellow villagers referred to him as *kotsingo,* "the strong one."

Wrestling, which is a daily activity of the Kuikuru, is done during the hottest part of the day. It is by no means a catch-as-catch-can affair, but has definite rules, not unlike those of Graeco-Roman wrestling.

It is their daily wrestling, which is carried out with great vigor, that brings out in men the very prominent muscles they are noted for.

Wrestling, which is called *kindene* by the Kuikuru, is more generally known in the Upper Xingú as *huka-huka*. This is the sound the wrestlers make as they circle each other just prior to locking arms and beginning to wrestle. It is said to imitate the roar of the jaguar.

I watched the Kuikuru wrestle many times and took numerous photographs of it, hoping to take one that would truly capture the straining of the wrestlers' powerful musculature, as well as the grips they use as they struggle for victory. The photo that most successfully did this —which I consider the third-best ethnographic photograph I ever took—enlarged to a healthy size, is affixed to the back of the sport exhibit case and dominates that section of the hall.

Before leaving Uluti I would like to take note of the fact that he was the only Indian I ever met who was even partially bald. The Kuikuru, who are always ready to manufacture an explanation for almost everything, attributed Uluti's baldness to his having eaten a great many piranha in his youth, the fish's razor sharp teeth having somehow nibbled away at his hair follicles.

I take the time to mention piranha here because their mandibls, bristling with blade-like teeth, were used by the Kuikuru to cut their hair before they had access to scissors. And I can attest to their working surprisingly well in doing this.

Since everyone knows about of the piranha's voracious appetite for anything that dares to venture near them in the water, I thought visitors would like to see, up close, the dental equipment which helps them satisfy that appetite. Accordingly, a couple of piranha mandibls are on display at opposite ends of the hall.

*   *   *   *

The exhibit on sports, as it was taking shape, was dominated by the imposing photograph of the Kuikuru wrestlers. But prominent as the wrestlers appeared in the enlarged photograph, they still were flat and two dimensional. Something was needed to fill in most of the empty space in the exhibit. I elected to do so by depicting the sport known as *javarí*. Now most of the exhibits in the South American hall are there because they are typical of at least certain tribes in Amazonia. *Javarí*, however, is different. It is there precisely because it is unique. Nowhere else on earth is this sport played than in the Upper Xingú in central Brazil. The most notable feature of it involves the use of the spear thrower, also known as the *atlatl*.

Historically, the spear thrower is distinctive because it was once of worldwide distribution as an important adjunct to the use of the spear in hunting.

When the Spaniards and Portuguese first sailed up the Amazon, hey saw the spear thrower being used by the Indians along that river to hunt the *pirarucú*, the world's largest fresh water fish. The device enabled a spear to be driven deeper into that fish's body than could be done by an arrow shot from a bow.

Around 15,000 years ago, though, the spear thrower began to be superseded by the bow and arrow in hunting. In South America it survives today only in *Javarí,* a sport which I will described shortly.

First though let me describe the spear thrower and its function. It is basically a shaft, usually of wood, with a handle at one end and a hook at the other which engages the butt end of a spear. When in use, a spear is laid on top of this shaft between the handle and the hook. With a strong forward thrust of the arm the spear disengages from the spear thrower and goes flying toward its target.

The advantage of the spear thrower is that It acts as an extension of the arm, helping to propel a spear faster and farther than the arm alone could do.

As I indicated above, the spear thrower now is found only in the Upper Xingú, where it still survives, but only with an altered function—or, more crrectly, with an altered *target* It is still used to propel a spear, not at a game animal but at a human being. The object is no longer to kill but to score points in a sporting event.

Javarí is a team sport, usually played between two villages. It is played by two men at a time who stand facing each other. Then the player on offense takes a few quick steps toward his opponent until he is within about fifteen feet from him, at which point he hurls his spear the aim of hitting him.

The defensive player tries his best to dodge the missile and in doing so can move his body but not his feet. He also makes use of a shield of sorts consisting of a bundle of slender sticks tied together.

After the offensive player has discharged his spear, the two men change sides, the offensive player now having to defend himself from his opponent's spear.

The combat continues until each man who is participating in it has had a chance to hurl his spear.

By all accounts *javarí* is a rough sport. Even though an effort is made to blunt the spear heads, propelled as they are at close range and with full force, broken bones do occur.

I never had a chance to witness *javarí*, which is played only occasionally. The Kuikuru however made me a spear thrower just like the ones they use in actual competition. I brought it back with me from the field and it now rests on the floor of the exhibit case devoted to Amazonian sports.

The artifact itself, though, is dwarfed by a blowup photograph showing the men of two Upper Xingú villages engaging in the sport.

Despite the paucity of artifacts in this exhibit case, the depiction of an actual *javarí* competition, along with the aforementioned photo of the wrestlers, makes this one of the more eye-catching exhibits in the hall.

*   *   *   *

After these digressions, let's return to puberty initiations for girls and take a close look at those of the Tikuna of the upper Amazon. And here we have an object lesson in the strength of imagination vs. the fallibility of memory—and what a quandary that can leave one in!

One paragraph below, presented *in extenso* and inside quotation marks, is my account of the puberty rite undergone by Tikuna girls as set forth in an earlier draft of this book. These remarks were based on what I thought was a clear recollection of what I had read about it, and here is what I said:

"Unlike those of the Kuikuru, the Initiation rites of Tikuna girls are among the most severe in all of Amazonia. And since we had in our collections virtually all the paraphernalia associated with it we took full advantage of it all and decided to have a display of this observance in all its harsh detail.

"The pubescent girl is first stupefied by having her drink large quantities of *chicha, a* fermented beverage, to lessen her pain, after which the older women pluck her bald, pulling out all her hair, strand by strand.

"Then the men have their innings with the girl. Dressed in grotesque bark cloth costumes impersonating evil spirits, and brandishing an enormous phallus, they go after the frightened girl. The hazing ends only when the men deem her to be sufficiently terrified. The ritual having been concluded, the girl is henceforth regarded as a woman."

And so the matter stood. Then one day, after having read over the label copy in the hall, Laila informed me that it did not accord with what I had written. And, as usual, she was right.

The label in this exhibit is actually a general statement about girls' puberty rituals in Amazonia generally. Virtually nothing is said in this label about the Tikuna puberty ritual specifically.

To tackle the problem of the inconsistency We then turned to the modern ethnographic accounts of the Tkuna by two highly regarded Brazilian ethnographers, Curt Nimuendajú and Harald Schultz. And their accounts paint a much softer picture of what a Tikuna girl goes through in her initiation than the one I had depicted. The hazing of the girl by men dressed in grotesque bark cloth costumes, and their brandishing of a huge phallus are not mentioned. Rather, they simply dance around her, making no Attempt to frighten her put of her wits.

What happened? Was it a case of my excogitation lurid details of this ceremony for their dramatic effect? That might appear to be the case but for the fact that the grotesque bark cloth costumes and the enormous phallus do in fact exist and are in the display. It seems unlikely, then, that I invented my version of events out of whole cloth. Could it be that many years ago, before they were studied by Nimuendajú and Schultz the Tikuna puberty rite was much more severe than it is now? Could it perhaps have been somewhat as I described it? Might they then have been true ordeals rather than simply rites?

But I am not trying to take refuge behind a convenient supposition. The matter has to be resolved, one way or another. It might be done by consulting Marcoy and other early 19tth-century sources—something that remains to be done.

* * * *

We had always expected to show segments of particularly good ethnographic films somewhere in the hall. But we thought we would be doing so in some darkened corner. But then we got a better idea—that of doing so in an alcove devoted solely to the showing films. It took a little reallocation of space but we managed it.

The area we chose for the alcove was nestled against the platform that held Andean archaeology. It gave us a fair amount of space, which enabled us to do pretty much what we wanted. It became possible to create a dark interior well suited for the projection of films. There was room for a couple of benches so that a dozen or more persons could sit while watched the films.

We took pains in choosing the films to be shown, selecting only the most interesting and informative parts of several films. All told we projected footage from parts of the best ethnographic films of Amazonian Indians we could find.

One of these segments consisted of some very well shot footage of a Guiana Indian woman processing bitter manioc, freeing it of its prussic acid content.

The star footage, though, is what I consider the best blowgun hunting sequence ever filmed. Moreover I can almost say that it was shot expressly for us. The film maker was Adrian Warren, head of the crack BBC documentary film unit. Warren was part of an expedition to the Waorani of eastern Ecuador organized by our great friend, Grant Behrman. Limited as we were in the length of footage we could show of any one film, we asked another great friend, Bob Dierbeck, a professional film editor, to cut our Waorani footage down to the most exciting parts. In a particularly riveting scene one can see Kampedi, a sixty-year-old Waorani, scampering through the treetops, pursuing a monkey he has just wounded.

All told we projected parts of some ten films, splicing together footage shot among several Amazonian tribes. Together they provided a full half-hour of viewing. At different times we were told by George Gardiner, head of the Exhibition department, and Tom Nicholson, director of the Museum, that this was too long, that no one would sit through that much film. We begged to differ, arguing that if the films were good enough—and we assured them they were—that at least a goodly number of persons would sit through them to the end.

And if need be, I'm sure I could find several people who would sign affidavits to that effect.

*   *   *   *

At the very beginning of the film alcove visitors will see the replica of a large rainforest tree, almost as if it were standing guard over the entrance to the alcove. My original intention was to journey to Manaos in the heart of the Brazilian rainforest and supervise the selection, cutting, and shipping of a section of the trunk of a big tree back to the Museum to show visitors what a tropical forest tree looks like.

But the great adventure I so looked forward to fell through even before it got started when I developed an ear infection. Recalling from past experience what misery it was to fly for hours with an earache, I reluctantly canceled the trip.

Fortunately, there was a Plan B to fall back on. There happened to be a sculptress named Jonquil Rock who had developed the specialty of making realistic replicas of trees, especially rainforest trees. I had seen examples of her work in the Bronx Zoo and the Central Park Zoo and had been impressed by it. So, after interviewing her and telling her what I was looking for, we hired her. It proved to be the right move for in a short time we had our tree. And there it stands today, its presence appearing to signal to visitors that something worthwhile is to be seen close by.

Standing stoutly as it does in front of the film alcove, our tree looked strong enough to withstand a gale force wind, but we were apprehensive that teenage fingernails would soon begin to disfigure it. So we contemplated surrounding it with a nice picket fence. But when I mentioned this to Jonquil she scoffed. The mixture of plastics she had used in creating her trees was such, she assured me, that even the claws of a jaguar could not mar it—or words to that effect.

And she was right. After thirty years of exposure to whatever New York City teenagers could bring to bear on its inviting surface—and without the protection of a picket fence—Jonquil's tree still looks pristine.

*   *   *   *

Throughout much of the hall we incorporated, as unobtrusively as possible, the artistry of our preparators. We would also have liked to show some of the Indians' own artwork, not anonymously but giving them full credit. Here though we faced a problem. Most of the Indians' artistry is lavished on their artifacts and on their persons as body decorations. There is virtually no "art for art's sake." Whatever objects they make that they—or we—may regard as beautiful is not made just to "look pretty." Almost invariably they also have some utilitarian function.

For this reason, there was virtually nothing in our collections that we could exhibit as an example of "pure art" from Amazonia.

So it was that in my slender file of Kuikuru art work there was next to nothing that would stand up to the test of being considered "serious art" by anyone's standards. Quite a bit of what I have in my files, in fact, may be put into the category of doodlings. (The Kuikuru term for this, more or less) is *kiriká*.) These doodlings can best be understood by knowing the circumstances under which they were made. Most of them were drawn at my request when I asked them to "draw something." Never did I dream that I might one day wish they would have turned out something more polished and substantial so that I might regard it as being of "museum quality"— something fit to be put on exhibit.

Two reasons, which I might go into, prompted me to ask the Kuikuru to "draw something." One was to see just how they visualized the *etseke*—spirits—of which they spoke so often.

The other reason was, frankly, to keep them occupied and out of my hair when I was trying hard to accomplish something. Occasionally, when a Kuikuru came down to my tent and I was busy, I would simply hand him a pencil and some paper and ask him to draw an *etseke,* or just anything that occurred to him. It was a good way to keep him busy, and occasionally—not often—it turned out to yield something I found nicely rendered.

One such occasion occurred when an informant, speaking of the Kuikuru afterworld, drew a picture of Ogomïgï, the dreaded two-headed vulture who was chief of the birds, living and dead, and who played a prominent role in Kuikuru mythology.

Ogomïgï had once been the owner of fire and had refused to share it with people, who had to wrest it from him by subterfuge.

Ogomïgï was also chief of the birds in the afterworld and as such led them into battle against the souls of dead Kuikuru. Whenever a Kuikuru soul was killed in the fighting, like a proper.vulture Ogomïgï would devour it.

In rummaging through my *kiriká* file I found what seemed to me a fine rendition of the fearsome Ogomïgï, drawn for me by some now-anonymous Kuikuru artist— whom I would gladly credit here if I could only remember his name.

When, during the installation of the hall, we got to the afterworld section, I asked one of our preparators to make a faithful copy of Ogomïgï as drawn by the Kuikuru artist, and it is this drawing that appears in the exhibit overlooking a fanciful map of the route followed by Kuikuru souls on their convoluted journey to the hereafter.

Incidentally the Kuikuru claim to have a greater knowledge of the afterworld than most peoples because, they say, while still living, a Kuikuru man visited his dead brother in the afterworld and returned to earth to tell people what it was like up there.

*   *   *   *

I have already said several times how much our exhibits were enhanced by the use of photographs, but I have not mentioned that a number of them were not from our photo archives but came to us thanks to the generosity and good will of of my fellow Amazonianists who knew we were working on the South American hall.

On a few happy occasions some of them happened to come by the Museum just as we were working on a particular exhibit they were associated with in some way. During one such occasion while I was standing in front of a case dealing with food preparation, I was joined by Helène and Philippe Erikson, who were on their way back to France from Brazil after doing field work with the Matsis. Helène noted that the display would be fuller if it had a photograph of a large cooking pot boiling merrily away on the fire. Moreover, she said, she happened to have such a photograph among her field photos which she had with her. Could we use it?

The photo—a color slide—was of an enormous pot boiling on an open fire inside an Indian house. Yes, we could use it.

I can report that today the photo of that pot, still boiling away, can be seen in the food preparation section of the hall.

Another example of a fellow Amazonianist donating something we could use in the hall was Tom Gregor's gift of an unusually large bullroarer—bigger than any I'd ever seen—which he'd collected among the Mehinaku of the Upper Xingú.

At the same time, we happened to have a photograph taken years earlier by the Brazilian ethnographer Harald Schultz which fitted right in with the exhibit we were working on. It depicted the strangely empty plaza of the Waurá village in the center of which a man stood whirling a large bullroarer over his head. Schultz' photograph and Gregor's bullroarer dovetailed nicely to form an intriguing exhibit unit.

The weird sound produced by a bullroarer as it is swung vigorously around is believed by many tribes—the Waurá being one—to be the voice of the spirits, which women and children are not allowed to see—accounted for their being kept indoors while the performance was taking place.

On another occasion a visiting Amazonianist, the ethnobotanist, Bill Balée, saved me from making a slight error. A label in the cordage and textile section, which we had all but completed, read that a certain type of cordage was made from *caraguatá*, a fiber which I had identified as coming from the wild pineapple plant. Bill, however, informed me that *caraguatá* was actually cultivated by a group he had worked with as well as several others he knew about. Thus it should not be considered a wild plant. Needless to say, I was happy to correct the label before we closed up the case.

*   *   *   *

During the installation of the hall I made no effort to keep track of the number of artifacts on exhibit that I myself had collected during my last two field trips, both of which can be considered Museum expeditions. They therefor formed part of the Museum's collections. Had I kept a tally of them the number would perhaps have come to a couple of dozen. Here I will name only one of those artifacts.

Would it be a large and impressive one like Winá's bow, which was so powerful I was unable to bring it to full draw? No, instead it will be a modest and inconspicuous object given to me by the Amahuaca—a tiny opossum cage, which was actually more of an open-mesh sack. When it came to me it was fully equipped with a baby opossum inside. I gave the little creature away but kept the cage which now hangs in the "House Interiors" section of the hall, along with such other items as fire fans and sitting mats, items that are likely to be found in virtually any Indian house.

Not that pet opossums are that common in native dwellings even though Amazonian Indians are quite ready to make a pet out of almost any animal, especially young ones. Their pets may range from a colorful macaw with two-foot-long tail feathers to a wriggly baby peccary, which a woman may nurse at her breast quite unselfconsciously.

This was not the first opossum I had received as a pet. The Kuikuru had given me one years before. I kept this one around my tent with a cord tied around its loins. One day, though, the opossum slipped his tether and ran away, ending up back in the village.

Now the Kuikuru like pets but play very roughly with them. Days later, when the Kuikuru returned the opossum to me, it was a changed animal. Once very docile, it was now hissing and scratching. The Kuikuru took it back but a few days later it was dead—no doubt teased to death by its owner.

I never learned what fate befell the opossum given to me by the Amahuaca, but I trust it met a more benign end.

*   *   *   *

I have played down my own contributions to the hall as far as artifacts are concerned. But I am not above trumpeting my photographs and what they add to the exhibits—especially those that depict an unusual and interesting event or activity, one rarely captured on film.

I don't pretend to be a great photographer; it's simply that, on rare occasions, circumstances have, placed me where uncommon events were taking place, and I was ready to record them with my Yashica twin lens reflex camera.

I have already spoken of my photograph of the wrestlers as being the third-best one of the field photos I have taken. The two more unusual ones I have in mind are ones that depict scenes virtually never get photographed—or even seen by field anthropologists.

The first, which is found toward the end of the "Life Cycle" section, is one phase of the Amahuaca's practice of funerary endocannibalism. It shows a woman sitting on the ground looking through a bowl containing the ashes of her infant daughter, who has just been cremated. The mother and her older daughter spent, by my watch, three hours and forty-five minutes carefully sifting through the infant's remains, looking for every little piece of bone and tooth they could find.

Later on, the woman ground these small fragments into a fine powder with a heavy mortar and pestle preparatory to mixing them with banana drink and ingesting them. By doing so, the Amahuaca believe, the remnants of the dear departed one will be kept close to the surviving relatives.

The other photograph I referred to is of a Kuikuru shaman attempting to effect the most dramatic and difficult act he is called upon to perform—the recovery of a missing soul.

The shaman, whose photograph can be seen in the "Religion" section of the hall, had diagnosed his patient's ailment as soul loss, resulting from an evil spirit having stolen it and taken it to the bottom of a lake. The shaman's task was to wrest the soul away from the evil spirit and re-implant it in the patient's body, thus restoring him to health.

In the scene captured in the photograph the shaman is seen blowing tobacco smoke on a straw doll called a *kefegé* in order to activate it so it can be used as a sort of magnet to draw the soul away from the spirit.

Unfortunately for the patient—but fortunately for me—the first soul recovery was a failure, meaning that the shaman had to go through the same procedure all over again. The first time I had been caught flat footed without my camera, but the second time I had some foreknowledge of what was coming and so I had my trusty Yashica at the ready, enabling me to take the photograph that now highlights the shamanism display.

(Incidentally the second attempt at soul recovery also failed, and so did the shaman's reputation as a curer. But that's another story.)

*   *   *   *

The following question may have reasonably arisen in some minds: If a museum curator is himself also a collector of artifacts does this not constitute—actually or potentially—a conflict of interest?.

It certainly may. Fortunately it has never created a problem for me since I am not a collector, at least not of objects connected with my job. Thus, I have never had the desire while I was in the field to collect

Indian artifacts for myself at the same time I was doing so for the Museum.

I can see the problem if one is in the field and comes across an artifact that is particularly beautiful or valuable but at the same time, absolutely unique s ... simply one of a kind. Do I collect it for me or for the Museum? Happily I have never had to struggle with that indecision.

In my apartment at home there are just two Amazonian Indian artifacts. One is a grating board from the Guianas which my wife took a fancy to and purchased in an Indian arts shop in Manaos. The other is a chief's stool given to me by the Kuikuru chief, Afukaká, once when he was brought to New York. But it was given with the understanding that it was meant for me personally and was not to be turned over to the Museum.

*　　*　　*　　*

That should put the question to rest. Still, let's pursue the matter a bit further. Suppose the earth suddenly stopped turning on its axis and that I developed a hankering to start collecting Indian artifacts from the Amazon. Where would I begin? Certainly I would not collect indiscriminately, wanting one of everything. Rather, I would be highly selective. I would collect only those objects that particularly interested me. And what would they be?

At the top of my list would be stone axes—if there were any left to collect in this day and age. Why would I choose this artifact above all others? Because the stone axe is emblematic of the way of life of the Indians of Amazonia before the arrival of Europeans. It best betokens their mode of subsistence—slash-and-burn agriculture— of which I have made a particular study. Indeed it continues to be so even if steel axes have replaced stone ones in clearing the forest.

There is something rugged and appealing about a way of life that relied on little more than human muscle power aided only by a polished stone blade attached to a stout handle.

The stone axe heads that the Amahuaca found for me in the bed of the Inuya River in eastern Peru were ones their ancestors had used not many years before. And in some very isolated corner of Amazonia today it is still possible that a tribe exists still relying on the stone axe.

We were fortunate when the time came to start working on the South American hall to have in our collections three genuine stone axes which, not long before, had been in the hands of men who felled trees with them. I was determined to display all three in the hall and to indicate their centrality to nabtive subsistence not many decades earlier. And, sure enough, today all three are mounted on the wall in the section devoted to subsistence. Two of them— one from the Nambikuara and the other from the Witoto—were already in our collections when I arrived at the Museum. The third one, however, which had been made by the recently-contacted Amarakaeri in southeastern Peru, I was instrumental in acquiring for the Museum.

It is a most interesting specimen in several ways. It is completely aboriginal in appearance in that no metal tools were used in crafting the handle to which the axe head is attached. Rather, it had been made by burning the opposite ends of a heavy tree limb.

This is shown by the fact that both ends of the limb that forms the handle were charred.

Isolated for years from contact with civilization, the Amarakaeri had been hostile to any outsiders who ventured into their territory. The first peaceful contact with them occurred in 1955 or thereabouts when a small group of them appeared unexpectedly at a newly established Catholic mission on the Colorado River in southeastern Peru. And to his good fortune this contact took place at the very moment that Tobias Schneebaum, an American artist on a Fulbright grant who had wandered down from the Andes, and appened to arrive at the mission himself.

The Amarakaeri had a few of their artifacts with them, including the aforementioned stone axe. Recognizing it as a very exotic object, Schneebaum had the good sense to trade for it. A friend of his, John Cohen, who had accompanied him on part of his journey in Peru and who had a good contact at the Museum, suggested to Schneebaum that he might be able to sell the stone axe to us.

The minute I laid eyes on that axe I knew we had to have it. I don't recall what we paid for it but I'm sure it wasn't nearly as much as I would have been willing to give for it had Schneebaum been inclined to bargain. I was determined to have that stone axe no matter what.

A few more words about Schneebaum seem in order. He took the first photographs ever taken of the Amarakaeri, copies of which now rest in my office. He befriended the few Amarakaeri he met at the mission and went with them back to their village, where he stayed for perhaps a couple of weeks.

Years later he wrote *Keep The River on Your Right,* a fanciful account of his stay with the Amarakaeri in which he sensationalized his experiences with them, painting them as living in the kind of native paradise he wished it to be.

Schneebaum's book became something of a cult classic—at least among those who shared his view of what a native paradise should be.

But returning to the stone axes in our exhibit, placed next to them are two small piles of wood chips, one of chips cut with a stone axe, the other of chips cut with a steel axe. I wanted visitors to be aware of the striking difference there is between chips of the two kinds. One set looks small and is rough hewn, much as I imagine chips gnawed off a tree by a beaver would look like.

In contrast, chips cut with a steel axe are distinctly larger, with a much cleaner, smoother surface.

What I would expect a visitor to take away from a comparison of the two sets of chips is how much more effort it must have taken to clear a garden plot with nothing but a stone axe.

Karl von den Steinen, a German ethnologist, who was the first outsider to enter the Upper Xingú, left a record of a charming little speech recited by a Bakairí Indian, complete with pantomime (which I have quoted elsewhere) of how much harder it was for him to topple a tree when only a stone axe was available to him.

* * * *

I have wandered off the trail on which I started when I began to tell the story of how the South American hall was put together. Let me try to pick up the thread again. And here I should say a few more words about Gene Bergmann—the designer whom the

Exhibition department had assigned to work with us, and the role he played in the layout of the hall.

While I had already decided on the segments into which Indian culture was to be divided, and in what order these segments were to be arrangedin the hall, Gene had much to do with exactly how the individual cases would be positioned and fitted together.

With regard to how our work proceeded, there was no master plan or schedule laid down from above, either by the director of the Museum or by the head of the Exhibition department. Day-to-day operations were entirely in our hands—"our" meaning Gene, Laila, and me.

As far as we knew, no one was looking over our shoulder, making sure we weren't doing anything wrong. It must have been thought that we knew what we were up to, and so we were left alone to continue doing as we were. It was a good atmosphere in which to work.

There was, however, one slight qualification to what I just said that deserves comment. Tom Nicholson, anticipating that during the installation of the hall issues would arise that would find Anthropology and Exhibition on opposite sides of the fence, and not wishing to ward them off and not to have to involve himself in our problems at every turn, issued the following edict. He told Gene and me,

"Gentlemen, there are curatorial decisions and design decisions and in making them each of you is to stay on his side of the fence."

Well, without ever really discussing this edict, Gene and I simply ignored it. Philosophically we didn't believe in it, so we just paid no attention to it. Whenever we had to deal with an issue concerning the exhibit Gene and Laila and I would resolve it ourselves. We talked it over until a consensus was reached. Never did we bother to ask ourselves whether it was a design decision or a curatorial one. "Jurisdictional disputes" simply never arose.

Now, getting wind, apparently, of the quiet way we had of handling every problem, and fearing perhaps that Laila and I were getting our way too often and that Exhibition's turf was thereby being trespassed on—maybe even trampled on— George Gardiner, the head of the Exhibition department, was heard to admonish Gene,

"Don't let Anthropology push you around."

We chuckled at this and continued to work together just as we had.

* * * *

Once the layout of the Hahn cases had been determined, the time had come for Laila and me to begin examining the "candidates" for exhibition, one by one, winnowing them down to those that would actually be put into the exhibit cases. And then we had to decide—with Gene's help—how best to arrange them inside each case.

After that, there was the matter of determining the order in which we would tackle the individual exhibits. After dealing with the introductory alcove, as already described, we did not follow any predetermined sequence. We dealt with whichever exhibit unit we wanted to work on next. Of course, it wasn't an altogether random process, but neither was it executed according to some preordained plan.

Of the 15,000 or so artifacts housed in our Amazonian store rooms we ended up with slightly more than 800 to be installed in our Hahn cases.

*   *   *   *

What we were displaying was, of course, an assortment of artifacts, which were once in active use but now lay there, inert. One way in which we could introduce the human element back into them was to put then into the hands, or onto the bodies, of, life-like manikins. Manikins had been used to good effect in the old South American hall, and in fact one of them had managed to survive the closure of that hall and was available for us to re-use should we choose to do so. It was the manikin of a Campa woman weaving a *cushma*, a long, nightshirt-like garment worn by several tribes in the Peruvian Montaña. In weaving the *cushma* the woman in the manikin was using a backstrap loom, an object we also wished to display.

But we also wanted some new manikins showing various activities, varying from the planting of manioc to a shaman treating his patient.

No one was left in the Exhibition department who could do this kind of work, so we had to turn to sculptors outside the Museum. One of them, Eliot Goldfinger, had once worked in the Museum before deciding to strike out on his own.

The procedure we established with the sculptors was for us to first talk to them individually, describing what activity we wanted his manikin to be engaged in, along with the pose we wanted the manikin to assume to best depict that activity. Also, what body type in a man or a woman he should look for in the model he was to use.

Beyond that, however we left it up to the sculptor to find the model on his own.

The quest for a suitable model led to some amusing incidents. On one occasion, spotting a man in a laundromat who seemed to be a good prospect, the sculptor approached him and asked if he would pose for him in skimpy bathing trunks. Thinking this had to be some kind of homosexual overture, the man picked up his clothes and ran off.

More memorable was the occasion when the sculptor—Eliot Goldfinger, in this instance—told us one day that he had found just the right model for the Guiana Indian woman planting manioc. Her name was Ra, he said, and she was half Spanish an half Pakistani. She had a metal chain soldered around her middle, he said, but added that he thought he could work around it. He then asked if he could bring her in so we could take a look at her. We didn't require the sculptors to do so but if Eliot wanted to bring her in we had no objection. "Sure," we said, "have her come in."

A couple of days later Eliot brought Ra into Laila's office, which was also our staging area. Without saying a word she proceeded to take off every stich of her clothing and stood before us, bare naked.

"Will I do?" she asked.

At that moment I could hardly have said no. Nor was there any need to do so since Ra was short and stocky, the very model of a Guiana Indian woman.

A little of the edge was taken off this experience when we learned shortly thereafter that Ra was an exotic dancer, so that disrobing in front of an audience was nothing special to her.

Be that as it may, you can see Ra in the flesh in the South American hall any day of the week, bending over at the waist as she inserts manioc cuttings into the ground.

The process of manikin making is an interesting one but is too lengthy to describe here in any detail. Basically it is this:

The model's body, once it has assumed the desired position, serves as the basis for a mold from which a plaster cast is made. The sculptor then uses his skill to build up or trim down the figure of the manikin until it approximates as closely as possible the figure we were looking for.

* * * *

I've kept referring to the sculptors as if they were all men because all but one of them was. In fact though one of them was a woman, Christin Nelson, who lived in San Francisco. (How we ever latched onto her I have no recollection.) At any rate the manikin we assigned to her was that of a shaman attempting to cure a sick girl. No new manikin was needed for the girl since one of a contorted girl was discovered somewhere in a back room of the Exhibition department, having once been used in some now-forgotten exhibit. The girl's contortions were quite appropriate since we wanted to show her lying in pain in her hammock, hoping for the shaman to work his wizardry on her.

Unlike the girl, the shaman's manikin had to be created new, and I made a special request of Christin to try to splay the toes of her manikin as much as possible. Why should I have done so with her I don't recall since I hadn't made the same request of any of the other sculptors, which I might well have.

The reason for doing so is simple. Amazonian Indians, since they wear no shoes, have toes that are not bunched together like ours, but are separated from each other. That is, they are splayed out.

The model Christin found for her shaman turned out to be a Nicaraguan weight lifter who lived in the Bay area. I suppose Christin did her best, but her manikin's toes still came out pretty bunched up.

That didn't really make much of a difference to me since I was sure not one visitor in a hundred would pay any attention to the shaman's feet. What their eyes were more likely to be drawn to was what the shaman was wearing—or *not* wearing—around his neck, namely, an item the Kuikuru refer to, In a sort of pidgin Portuguese, as an "onça colar," that is, a jaguar claw necklace.

Since this necklace is made up of the claws of two or more jaguars, and since killing even one jaguar is a feat of skill and courage, it is no wonder that jaguar claw necklaces are so highly prized, and that not every man in the village had one.

Now, almost all of the artifacts on exhibit in the South American hall were already in our possession when we began installingit. Not so with the jaguar claw necklace the visitor will see hanging from the shaman's neck. How it came to be there … how we managed to acquire this one is a story worth telling.

During my first visit to the Kuikuru village I soon became aware of this necklace and of the great esteem in which it was held. It is the most valuable thing they have. Thus it became one of their artifacts I most wanted to obtain. Yet I was never able to do so. The asking price was always higher than I could meet with my limited supply of trade goods.

On one occasion, though, I thought I was on the verge of obtaining one. But in the end I was foiled. It happened in this way.

Back in 1954 my wife, Gertude Dole, and I lived in a tent just outside the Kuikuru village. We slept in hammocks but had a cot which we sat while eating our meals. We told the Kuikuru that we did not wish to have anyone enter our tent while we were away, and for the most part they respected this.

Then one day, upon returning to the tent, we found a number of red splotches on the cot. Without a doubt the splotches had been made by the ever-present *urucú* with which the Kuikuru, like most Amazonian tribes, paint their bodies.

Ready as they are to tell on each other, the Kuikuru soon let us know that the red marks had been made by Juafiká and

Agisoka, a young couple who had evidently found our cot an inviting *lit d'amour*.

This posed a problem for me. On the one hand, while I didn't want my wishes regarding entering the tent to be flouted, I also wanted to avoid the unpleasantness of confronting Juafiká about the matter.

And leasr of all I didn't relish the prospect of returning to the tent unexpectedly one day and finding the couple *in flagrante delictu.*

What to do?

Slowly a clever scheme began to take shape in my mind. Juafiká was one of the few Kuikuru who owned a jaguar claw necklace, and thereby—I thought—lay the solution to all my problems.

A day or two later I approached Juafiká and, looking at him with my most meaningful leer, gave him to know that the jig was u, that I had found him out.

Then my expression changed to one of the greatest benignity. I told him I knew that he and Agisoka enjoyed our cot and that I had a deal to propose to him that I thought he would like. I said I was ready to make the following exchange with him. When we were ready to leave the village for good, I would turn the cot over to him in exchange for his jaguar claw necklace.

Juafiká gave me a sheepish grin at having been discovered, and then agreed to the deal.

Now, I had never had the intention of taking the cot back to civilization with me so I thought the deal was pure profit for me. I was giving up nothing I intended to keep so it would be getting something I very much wanted for nothing. I smiled inwardly at my own ingenuity.

The day we left the Kuikuru for good was a festive one. To wish us goodbye everyone in the village was down at the canoe port from which we would be leaving. Everyone, that is, except Juafiká. He figured—correctly—that I was not about to overload our already jam-packed canoe with our cot, just to keep him from getting it if he failed to come through with his end of the bargain. All he had to do, therefor, was stay out of sight for a couple of hours and the cot was his without having to give up his precious necklace.

And he was right. He had out-foxed the fox.

Skip ahead now a few decades to around 1988 when the South American hall was in its final stages of installation. I was standing in front of the manikin of the shaman treating the sick girl, in his hand a gourd rattle, an adjunct to shamanic curing, around his neck ... nothing.

Standing next to me that day was Emi Ireland, an Amazonian ethnologist whose field work had been among the Waurá, neighbors of the Kuikuru in the Upper Xingú. I must have told her the story of how close I thought I had come to acquiring a jaguar claw necklace only to be outsmarted by someone I thought I had gotten the better of.

Imagine my surprise—and delight—when Emi suddenly told me she had obtained a jaguar claw necklace from the Waurá and that she was willing to donate it to the Museum. But there was a condition to her offer: that we were not put the necklace in a store room but would place it on exhibit in the hall, where it would remain for the whole world to see.

You can imagine the alacrity with which I accepted her offer, happily acceding to her condition.

So today that "onça colar" hangs around the shaman's neck for visitors to admire as he does his best to cure the sick girl. What they never think of doing is complaining about his toes being bunched up.

And neither do they have the slightest idea of the convoluted series of events that led up to his having that jaguar claw necklace around his neck.

*   *   *   *

Amazonia is one of the great drug taking areas of the world. Perhaps the greatest. That being the case, we certainly had to include this aspect of Amazonian Indian culture in our exhibit. Moreover, we felt that what we had in the store rooms in the way of drug taking paraphernalia was sufficient to do justice to an exhibitof the practice.

In the section of the hall immediately to the left of the shaman, visitors are confronted with a striking photograph by Ken Good showing a Yanomamö holding a long tube up to the nose of another man in the act of blowing *paricá* snuff up the man's nostrils. The latter's facial expression indicates that he is steeling himself for the charge he is about to receive. Some snuff taking tribes use a small v-shaped tube— shown in the exhibit—which allows a man to blow snuff up his own nose.

Although not always thought of as a narcotic, tobacco nevertheless belongs in the family of substances that are ingested but have nothing to do with nutrition. As such, tobacco deserves a place in this section. And again, we thought we had material enough to deal with it.

Being the area of the world where tobacco was first domesticated, it is not surprising that Amazonia is also the area where we find a variety of ways of smoking it. Most often it is done in the form of cigars or cigarettes, but it is also smoked in pipes. An Amahuaca pipe, here displayed, is made from the stem of a slender palm tree, the bowl of the pipe being made by hollowing out the pith center of the palm stem.

I'm prepared to wager that not even the most dedicated two-pack-a-day smoker has ever seen a tobacco seed. They are tiny, being less than half a millimeter in diameter. Hundreds of them are found inside the pod in which they grow. We had some in our collections and they went into the exhibit.

Among many Amazonian tribes the use of tobacco is an important adjunct of a shaman's practice. Indeed, among some groups, like the Kuikuru, smoking is a prerogative of the shaman, other men rarely doing so.

An important source of drugs in Amazonia—and elsewhere in the New World—is the genus *Datura,* various species of which—like the one known in North America as jimson weed—are taken for their narcotic effects. The Jívaro, for instance, take *Daatura* at night to keep themselves awake when they are expecting an enemy raid.

But the Amazonian narcotic that has come into greatest notoriety recently is *ayahuasca,* derived from the vine *Banisteriopsis caapi.* We happened to have a thick stem of this vine store rooms and it too is in the exhibit.

This hallucinogenic drug has become so well known in this country that today there are *ayahuasca* parties in California.

This narcotic produces very vivid, colorful, and often frightening hallucinations. Novice takers of the drug in Amazonia often report such experiences as seeing snakes crawling up their legs.

Ayahuasca was first made known in the U.S. when the New Age writer William Burroughs (*Naked Lunch*) experimented with it in Colombia and wrote about its effects to his friend Allen Ginsberg, urging him to come down and try it. Their correspondence was later published in a book entitled *The Yage Letters,* "yage" being another name for *ayahuasca.*

When I was in the jungle town of Pucallpa in Peru in 1960 I was told about a crazy American poet who had been in town the year before. Needless to say, the "crazy American poet," tuned out to be Ginsberg, who had followed his friend's advice to experiment with it.

Some years later, I had been reading a book about travels in Amazonia which contained an account of a tribe which took *ayahuasca*, not orally, as is usually done, but rectally. I was struck by this practice which I had never read of before.

It just so happened that that very afternoon a nurse came in to see me about some other matter and, with what I'd just read still fresh in my mind, I bubbled over to her about the odd custom.

Without batting an eye she proceed to rattle off three good reasons for taking *ayahuasca* in this fashion:

(1)   Its hallucinogenic effects would be felt more quickly.

(2)   It avoided the nausea that generally accompanies the taking of *ayahuasca* by mouth

(3)   By bypassing the liver, the denaturing function of that organ is bypassed.

I was so impressed by the nurse's ready knowledge of human physiology that I hardly knew how to respond.

(I should add that I have since learned that this knowledge of the most effective way of taking *ayahuasca* has reached California and is being put into practice there too.)

I am not sure of this but I think the book in which I read about the rectal administering of *ayahuasca* was the one written by Herndon and Gibbon ... and thereby hangs a tale.

In the 1840s word reached the U.S. Congress that there were commercial possibilities in Amazonia that deserved to be explored. Accordingly, Congress commissioned two naval officers, lieutenants Herndon and Gibbon, to go to the Amazon, investigate these possibilities, and report back their findings. They did so and the result was a two-volume work published in 1851. They found that indeed there was money to be made in Amazonia, principally by trading in coca leaves.

Back in Hannibal, Missouri, Herndon and Gibbon's book somehow fell nto the hands of Mark Twain (then still only Samuel Clemons) whose imagination was fired by the prospect of making his fortune in the Amazon.

Not generally known, even to dyed-in-the-wool Mark Twain buffs, is the reason Mark Twain went down the Mississippi River in the first place. It was his intention to reach New Orleans and there to book passage on a ship bound for Brazil and the Amazon. Alas, there was no ship leaving New Orleans for Brazil, either then or in the foreseeable future. So Twain went back up the Mississippi, apprenticed himself to Horace Bixby, and under his tutelage learned how to pilot a boat on the Mississippi River. The rest, as they say, is history.

But it is interesting to speculate along these lines: Suppose there had been a ship in New Orleans bound for Brazil ... who knows, instead of *Life on the Mississippi* we might have had *Life on the Amazon*.

* * * *

One day the Schwartz brothers, who had made most of the manikins for the hall, approached me with a request. Could they make a manikin of me?

It seemed that the Steelcase Company, a leading manufacturer of office furniture, had commissioned them to make some two dozen manikins for a large trade fair to be held in Chicago. One of the manikins the Schwartz brothers had been asked to make was of a middle aged businessman leaning back in his chair with his feet on his desk, leafing through a travel brochure as he contemplating his forthcoming vacation. The Schwartz brothers felt that I looked the part and asked me if I would serve as a model for the manikin. I readily agreed. Here was my chance, I thought, for a bit of immortality!

Ready for my first modeling job, I appeared the next morning at the Schwartz' studio in Brooklyn with my bathing trunks under my pants. Shortly after arriving I stripped down to my trunks and stood there as three young women opened an enormous jar of vaseline and proceeded to slather me all over with a thick coating of the stuff, the idea being to keep the hair on my body from sticking to the plaster of Paris in which I was soon to be encased.

Two tiny holes were left for my nostrils so I could breathe while I rested inside my cocoon. Then swatches of what looked like heavy gauze that had been impregnated with plaster of Paris were dipped into a bucket of water and then carefully, layer after layer, laid over every square inch of me. I was asked to remain motionless to give the plaster time to set.

Some minutes later the swatches were peeled off my body and later reassembled to create a mold from which a cast of me was made. And there I was, re-created in plaster, ready to play my role of businessman-looking- forward-to-a-vacation.

Had you been in Chicago some time in the 1990s and visited a trade fair of office furniture, and happened to stop by the Steelcase exhibit ….

*　*　*　*

I've already mentioned that we salvaged a manikin from the old South American hall and reused it in the new hall. It was, as I said, that of a woman weaving a *cushma* on a backstrap loom. That loom deserves further comment. In front of the weaver as she sat at her task in the exhibit, I decided to place a copy of the best illustration of this type of loom I have ever seen. Every part of it is shown with great clarity and precision so that it is easy to visualize just what function each part performs when the loom is in use. illustrations of this quality are particularly valuable whenever an implement of even moderate complexity is being exhibited. This Illustration comes from Bennett and Bird's *Andean Culture History,* my textbook when I took a course on South American prehistory as a graduate student. I distinctly remember admiring it the first time I saw it but never did I imagine that some day I would have occasion to make good use of it in an exhibit. Still, it had never left my mind and when the opportunity arose to make use of it I took full advantage of it. I asked a preparator to make an exact copy of it for the weaving exhibit.

*　　*　　*　　*

Two other manikins in the hall deserve extended remarks. They are in separate exhibit cases quite some distance from each other but in real life they represent an Amahuaca couple, Winá and his wife Kï'o. Had you taken a poll of the Amahuaca community in which they lived and asked which among them was the most admired couple, Winá and Kï'o would have won hands down.

In the hall the two appear portraying very different activities, Winá, in the pose of a hunter drawing a bow so powerful, as I noted earlier, that I was unable to bring it to full draw.

Kï'o is shown planting maize, and at first glance you might suppose that that is why she is standing with a digging stick in her hand. But you would be mistaken. To discover the real reason I wanted her there look up at the outside of the case and you will see that she is in the "Adornment" section of the hall, and that is why she is there, wearing the most beautifully crafted headdress I have ever seen. In a way I feel that I stole that headdress from her because I got it in exchange for an Estwing all-steel hatchet that you can buy in any good hardware store, whereas her headdress is an absolutely unique piece and must have taken hundreds of hours to make. No Indian headdress I have ever seen comes even close to it in the artistry of its design or the skill in its execution.

I salve my conscience for having taken it away from Kï'o by recalling the look in her eyes when we made the exchange, a look that seemed to say that she felt she had gotten the better of the deal. However, I still have the feeling that I deprived her of that magnificent headdress which will never again adorn that noble brow.

Unfortunately, the viewer will not have seen Ki'o's headdress in all its pristine beauty. It had to travel thousands of miles to get here and it bears some marks of its long journey. Still, it is a majestic example of Amazonian Indian art and deserves every accolade I have bestowed on it.

I cannot resist adding a few more words of praise on this headdress. Its beauty is not of the spectacular kind. It does not strike one as stunning. Rathe, its beauty is more of a subtle and delicate nature, one which comes through from quiet and close contemplation of how it must have been put together.

But enough of encomiums. Let me make an attempt to describe what it looks like.

…. I have tried several times to do so but each attempt has fallen short. And rather than present an inadequate description of something so special that it demands to be done with corresponding artistry, it is best to forego any further attempts in that direction. It will have to be seen.

I never learned who made this headdress but I assume it was Winá, her husband, an accomplished artisan who made it as a token of his affection.

Just one more word about Kï'o. She was the most graceful Indian woman I have ever seen. I can still visualize her spinning cotton, extending her right arm out to the side in a grand sweeping gesture as she slowly unwound the spun thread from her spindle.

* * * *

Besides the manikin of the Campa woman weaving a *cushma* and the manikin of the contorted girl, we salvaged one other item from past exhibits which we found reason to incorporate into the new hall. This was a carefully made set of miniature hunting traps which showed very nicely the kinds of traps used by tribes who rely heavily on game animals in their subsistence.

At first I erroneously thought these delicate little models had been made for the old South American hall, but Laila, researching the matter, discovered that they had actually formed part of the "Men of the Montaña" exhibit and had been saved when that temporary exhibit had finally closed after being open for more than twenty years.

Several kinds of traps were included in this set. One of them consists of a box-like cage that, when its activating mechanism is tripped, falls on the unsuspecting animal, holding it securely until the hunter can come and dispatch it.

Another type of trap, called a dead fall, operates in such a way that when tripped it drops a heavy log on the animal's head, crushing its skull.

We used all these models in the new hall but the one which really caught my fancy was the spring pole snare in which the stout limb of a standing tree is pulled back and has a sharp dagger attached to its end. When the trigger mechanism of this trap is set off, the bent branch springs forward with great force, driving the dagger deep into the animal that set it off.

I say "animal" but in fact it is more often a human being who sets it off. This is so because the device is used by tribes frequently at war in an effort to safeguard their village against enemy attack.

The business end of a full size spring pole trap is on display in the warfare section of the exhibit, having been collected for us by Michael Harner among the Jívaro who have good reason to use it.

One day I was showing the hall to an ex-GI who had fought in Vietnam and was told by him that the same type of weapon was employed by the Vietcong in carrying on jungle warfare.

*   *   *   *

Amazonia is not noted for its musical culture. The types of musical instruments used are limited, the most common type being the flute. Almost every tribe has some kind of flute, often several kinds. The Kuikuru, for instance, have nine different kinds of flute.

With one exception—to be noted shortly—flute playing is usually a casual matter as far as the flute player is concerned. To show just how relaxed it can be we have used a photograph in the "Music" section that clearly suggests this. It shows a young man perched on the lower limb of a tree playing his flute, the expression on his face indicating how completely satisfied with himself he seems to be.

The serious flute playing I alluded to involves the use of a class of instruments loosely referred to as "sacred flutes". They are sacred only in the sense that women are not allowed to see them under some kind of penalty. In the Upper Xingú the penalty is a severe one—gang rape.

The sacred flutes I am familiar with are those used by the Kuikuru. They are not hollow bamboo tubes as Anazonian flutes generally are, but are carved from a hard, heavy wood. The two halves are carved separately and then affixed together.

They are played in threes, usually at night, and often all night long. They have a most lugubrious sound which I can still hear in my head even after 65 years of not having actually heard them.

Alas, they do not appear in the exhibit although I would dearly have liked to have them to display and to tell their misogynist story in the label copy. As in the case of the jaguar claw necklace, I came close to acquiring one while I was in the field but missed out by a hair.

No such dramatic episode surrounded this failure as did the jaguar claw necklace but I'll recount it anyway.

I first heard the sacred flutes when I entered the Kuikuru village in 1953. It didn't take long for me to become familiar with them and to develop a hearty dislike for their unearthly sound. Thus I was pleased to learn on my return to the Kuikuru more than twenty years later that there were no sacred flutes left in the village. Their owner, Faifuá, had died since my first visit to the village and after his death, following Kuikuru custom, his flutes, along with the rest of his material possessions, were destroyed.

Talá, an excellent craftsman who had made the flutes, and the only man in the village who knew how, apparently to honor the memory of his old friend, had chosen not to make another set.

Yet, much to my surprise, Talá offered to make me a sacred flute in exchange for a bar of *rapadura,* a brown sugar candy which he evidently had once tasted and for which he'd developed an inordinate fondness. I had brought a couple of bars of *rapadura* with me into the field, but only for my own delectation, unaware that it might prove to be of inestimable value as a trade item.

Unfortunately, I had just finished eating my last bar, quite oblivious to what I might have gotten in exchange for it.

What we do have on exhibit in the "Music" section, far removed from where the sacred flute would have been, is a delicate little musical bow. The Amahuaca, from whom I acquired it, are one of only three tribes in all of Amazonia to have such an instrument. It is bowed rather than plucked, as are musical bows elsewhere in the world. The Amahuaca bow is played by placing one end in the mouth, the oral cavity acting as a resonating chamber, magnifying the bow's tiny sound.

At the very opposite end of the scale of musical instruments in terms of size and strength of sound is the slit log drum, one of which we have in our store rooms.

Actually, it is questionable whether one should even refer to the slit log drum as a musical instrument since its principal function is to signal from one village to another, especially to warn a neighbor of an impending enemy attack.

The slit log drum, popularly referred to as a tom-tom, has a deep, booming sound which is said to carry for ten miles through the jungle. It is made from a single tree trunk which may be as much as three feet thick. It is hollowed out by alternately burning and chopping until the desired shape and sound is achieved. The drum in our collection is relatively small but it probably could give a good account of itself.

Nor was I the only one to think so. Just listen.

At one time it occurred to me to place our slit log drum in the anterior portion of the South American hall (Section 6) and to attach to it a pair of drumsticks, allowing visitors to get a feel for what it must be like to live in an Indian village contemplating an impending an attack.

However, the editorial offices of *Natural History* magazine were at that time located a thin wall away from where I proposed to set up the drum. And when the editors of the magazine got wind of my intention they pleaded for mercy, arguing that they would be driven mad by the incessant pounding they expected to hear from exuberant visitors enjoying a rare opportunity.

Their concerns were communicated to me and, being the kind- hearted soul that I am, I relented. And without the drumstick to bring it to life, I saw little point in bringing the slit log drum out of its store room.

* * * *

It was the mid-1980s and the feminist movement was at its height. Seeing an opportunity to show my support for it, I conceived of a way to do so. It would be in a small exhibit space just beyond the "Music" section and would take the form of a drinking bout. The conception was brilliant, but the execution fizzled.

Here is the scene. The drinking bout is taking place inside a house, with the residents already deep in their cups and, as is usual on such occasions, the social constraints greatly relaxed. In the darkened doorway of the house one can discern a woman wrestling with a man, trying hard to drag him outside into the bushes, with— one can only guess—what intent.

But the house is small and the light dim, so that a visitor can hardly make out the couple in the doorway, let alone tell who is the man and who is the woman. Thus— alas—it is all but impossible for him to grasp what message the curator intended to convey.

But, as they say, it's the thought that counts.

* * * *

I have already noted motr than once how, on occasion, in the course of preparing the South American hall, I have benefited from the experience, resources, and good will of my fellow Amazonianists. Here I would like to present one more example of such help, this one a particularly good one.

Just around the time we were working on ceremonies and the costumes associated with them, I happened to receive a copy of the FUNAI magazine. (FUNAI is the Brazilian agency in charge of Indian affairs.) The cover of this issue showed a Bakairí Indian dressed in a very handsome costume, one which I would have liked to include in our exhibit. I had never seen this costume before and was sure we did not have one in our collections. However, an idea came to me of how we might be able to obtain one.

I was acquainted with Debra Picchi, an Amazonianist who had done field work with the same Bakairí whose cotume was on the cover of the magazine. Accordingly, I wrote to Debra and asked if she could possibly arrange to obtain one of those costumes for us to exhibit in the South American hall the next time she went into the field. She replied that she thought she could arrange it.

Some weeks later she informed me that the Bakairí were willing to make the costume for us but wanted the equivalent of about ninety dollars'worth of trade goods for the work. That was easy enough to arrange but there was another condition that had to be met before the transaction could be concluded.

The costume I wanted was worn in a ceremony that women weren't allowed to see. Debra told the Bakairí that where the costume was going women would indeed be seeing it. By means I never asked her about—nor did she divulge them to me—Debra was able to get the Bakairí to waive the customary restriction. As a result, that costume is now on display in the Museum, visible, without qualms, to any pair of eyes.

*   *   *   *

Just beyond the Bkairí costume in the hall the visitor comes to what is probably the best known ceremony of Amazonian Indians—*kuarup,* the feast of the dead, celebrated by the Indians of the Upper Xingú.

As a measure of how well known this ceremony has become, the year I saw it performed—1975—it was witnessed by the president of FUNAI as well as four foreign ambassadors.

This ceremony, which takes place during the dry season, cycles among the nine villages of the Upper Xingú so that, on the average, each village holds it every ninth year. The host village sets up a memorial post for each member of the chiefly line from that village who has died since it last hosted it.

The memorial posts, which are massive, each represents a particular individual. They are cut from a special tree, *uengufi*, which is associated with chiefs. The posts, which are about 6 feet long, are stripped of their bark over a length of about two feet, and this section is decorated with traditional designs. The upper end of each post has a cotton headdress wrapped around it into which three or four macaw tail feathers are inserted.

The posts are heavy, which accounts for their never having been brought out of the Upper Xingú. Thus, if I wanted to exhibit them in the hall—which I certainly did, since they are the major focus of the *kuarup* ceremony—I would have to have them duplicated by the preparators in the Exhibition department.

This was done very skillfully, and in fact constitutes one of the best examples of the preparator's art that we have in the hall.

*   *   *   *

It was always my objective, as I have stated before, to exhibit only the aboriginal culture of Amazonia. After all, who would come to our exhibit to see a man dressed in a Notre DameT-shirt (which I once saw in the highlands of New Guinea) and wearing a pair of tennis shoes, or a woman with a string of cheap glass beads around her neck and her breasts encased in a bràssiere? We always assumed that what people would most like to see was the traditional Indian culture. If not in our Museum, where else could they see it?

The Museum of the American Indian was moving to Washington, D.C. and besides, under their new management, were going in a different direction with their exhibits.

And so we planned and executed the hall according to the philosophy I just described.

Furthermore, it was the native culture that we were best equipped to exhibit—as good or better than any other museum in the country.

Now, at the same time, we made no effort to hide the fact that most Amazonian tribes today have been greatly modified by their contact with Western civilization. But while not denying this fact we had no interest in trumpeting it. Let some other museum display Amazonian Indian culture as it has been transformed by acculturation if they chose to do so. We would stick to the aboriginal culture as closely as we could.

That is why I shed hardly a tear when the Fire Department insisted that we build a new fire exit in a small corner of the hall we had tentatively assigned to a modest exhibit case on acculturation.

*   *   *   *

I have just state that in presenting Amazonian Indian culture we have stuck to the aboriginal "as closely as we could." That phrase was meant to offer a loophole, allowing for the possibility of their being occasional exceptions, (rare as they might be) to the rule we had set for ourselves. The most notable instance of such an exception occurs in the "Adornment" case and involves the trapezoidal pubic apron—sometimes called a *tanga*—worn by many Indian women in the Guianas. In virtually every case these little aprons—always very neatly crafted—are made using glass beads of made in Czechoslovakia. These beads, the best glass beads made anywhere, have been used in the Guianas for decorative purposes for at least two centuries.

The pubic apron was originally made of seed beads derived from a variety of trees in the surrounding forests, and we included one of them in the "Adornment" section to show the aboriginal prototype of the present day *tanga*.

Once high quality glass beads had flooded the Guianas, it became much easier to fashion *tangas* from them than from the native seed beads, which had to be laboriously gathered in the surrounding forest. In time glass bead *tangas* had completely superseded the native ones, becoming recognized as virtually the standard attire of Guiana Indian women, even while other elements of the native culture were being retained.

Accordingly, we decided to award glass bead *tangas* honorary aboriginal status and to exhibit them in the adornment case without apology.

*   *   *   *

It was about time I said more about the anterior part of the South American hall –Section 6—which, despite my making light of it now and then, was actually a significant part of the hall. It was something of a mish-mosh of archaeology and ethnolog.

To it I had consigned the cultures of the Chaco, Pampas- Patagonia, and Tierra del Fuego, leaving Section 8—my half of it anyway—for exhibiting the tribes of

Amazonia, where, as I have noted before, the strength of our collections lay, as well as being the region of the continent I was most familiar with, having dome my field work there.

At the very beginning of Section 6, where the visitor first sets foot inside the hall, we placed a map of South America showing the culture areas into which anthropologists have divided the continent. In this regard, one day a Brazilian naval officer visiting the hall complained that we had drawn Amazonia too large. It was necessary to explain to him that Brazilians, especially when speaking in political terms, often restricted the region to what is called "Amazonia legal," an area whose inhabitants are entitled to certain government subsidies as a way of attracting settlement of the interior of Brazil.

Anthropologists, on the other hand, think of Amazonia more broadly, as encompassing virtually all of lowland tropical South America, with the West Indies sometimes being thrown in for good measure—an area which shared a certain type of culture with the mainland with a subsistence base depending on slash-and-burn cultivation, having manioc as the principal crop.

Once inside the hall, visitors would notice on the wall to their left what I think may be an innovation in ethnographic exhibits. The entire expanse of this wall is covered by a huge mural depicting a broad expanse of rainforest. On the floor directly in front of the mural we placed an assortment of artifacts, each derived from some plant or animal pictured on the mural. Adjacent to the artifacts on the floor a sketch map shows just where on the mural the plant or animal from which the artifact was derived can be seen.

The idea behind this exhibit was to show the extent to which Amazonian Indians rely on the flora and fauna of their habitat for their subsistence needs and their material culture.

To cite just a few examples of things that are derived from the plants or animals that can be seen on the mural:

From the Brazil nut tree, the tallest tree in the forest, the Indians obtain an edible nut (which the Yanomamö crack open with their teeth) and which has the highest fat content of any nut.

From the profusion of birds that perch high on the upper branches of the trees they pluck beautiful feathers, like those of the macaw and cotinga, with which they fashion their colorful headdresses.

From the bamboo which grows interspersed amidst the larger trees of the forest they derive sharp, serrated, knives which, being sterile when freshly obtained, are used to cut the umbilical cords of their newborn.

And from piranha mandibles (not shown on the mural) studded as they are with razor sharp teeth, they obtained an implement what was used for other forms of cutting before knives and scissors became available to them.

Altogether there are some fifty or so artifacts scattered around in this exhibit testifying to the enormous versatility of the rainforest as a source of many things that support or enhance life.

The artist who painted this mural, Barron Storey, I discovered while leafing through the pages of the *National Geographic*. On two occasions he had rendered tropical rainforest backgrounds to article in the magazine and I had liked his work. There was a deftness to his depiction of the rainforest, with each tree retaining its individuality among so many others in a way I admired. When the idea of a mural for the hall occurred to me, therefor, I knew whom I wanted to paint it. We hired Barron and were greatly pleased with the results. The mural provided a rich background for displaying the wide range of forest products drawn on by Amazonian Indians.

Barron lived in San Francisco but came to New York to discuss what the work on the mural would entail, returning here several times during the course of the project.

Most of the work was actually carried out in his studio in San Francisco before the mural was finally transferred to the wall in the South American hall.

* * * *

While Barron was here we became friends and had a number of pleasant lunches together. During these we discussed, among other things, a topic that on occasion comes up in conversations between scientists and artists, and which usually finds them on opposite sides: free will vs. determinism. Barron championed free will, while I upheld determinism.

The time came for Barron to return to San Francisco for good, but we continued debating the issue by mail. In my last letter to him, trying again to turn him from his position to mine, I argued as follows:

"Wouldn't you rather have your will be a summation and expression of everything that has gone into you, making you what you are, rather than having your will be a result of random factors, completely unrelated to your life experiences?"

I never learned if this line of argument carried any weight with him since I never heard from him again.

* * * *

Let me turn attention now to the extreme southwest corner of the South American hall. In apportioning space, this area fell to Craig, hence It was up to him to come up with some idea of what was to be displayed there. Initially he had decided to hang a series of banners from the ceiling decorated with Inca-like designs. I don't think Craig was ever really happy with the banners and when an opportunity presented itself to replace them with something more authentically emblematic of prehistoric Peru, he seized it. The exhibit to replace the banners, which was to be only temporary was called *Lords of Sipán,* and consisted of a replica of a royal tomb recently excavated on the coast of Peru. The replica of the tomb was painstakingly constructed by our preparators based on notes, maps, and photographs provided by the excavators of Sipán.

The grave goods we showed in the tomb were not replicas but the very ones found in the tomb, which were loaned to us for the exhibit and included some gold objects with which the royal personage had been buried.

After a year or two the artifacts were returned to Peru, but the replica of the tomb remained as a permanent part of the exhibit.

* * * *

If it had been my choice as to what to do with that corner of the hall once the spectacular part of the exhibit went back to Peru, it would have been—needless to say—something Amazonian instead of Andean. I had in fact already thought about it a good deal. And here is what I would have liked to see in that southwest corner of the hall.

Imagine a large rainforest tree sculpted by the one-and-only Jonquil Rock looking as if It were growing out of the floor. The tree would have prominent plank buttress roots above which a scaffold had been built. Standing on this scaffold two men would be seen wielding their stone axes. One of them would just have landed a heavy blow on the trunk of the tree while the other would be poised with his axe upraised, about to deliver a heavy blow himself.

This scene, as I pictured it, would have captured a moment of dynamic tension in a process repeated countless times in the cycle of slash-and-burn cultivation by which Amazonian Indians have long subsisted.

Better than any other, this scene would have caught the eye of a visitor the moment he set foot in the hall–Which is, after all what we would have wanted to do.

*   *   *   *

But the southwestern corner of the hall remains securely in the hands of archaeology whose youngest object on exhibit is at least five centuries older than the oldest object in the ethnographic sections. Which is admittedly an awkward way of bringing up the question of which is the oldest ethnographic artifact on exhibit. Unless there is an older one which escapes my memory at the moment it would have to be the Mundurucú head located in the "Warfare" section. This object is a war trophy, and even though it is generally known as a Mundurucú head, and despite the fact that the Mundurucú did in fact prepare it, the head itself is almost certainly that of a Kayapó, the traditional enemies of the Mundurucú. It is said that a Mundurucú war party would walk as far as two hundred miles in order to find a Kayapó village to raid.

My belief that the trophy head is that of a Kayapó is based on the fact that the head on display in our exhibit is shaved back to the crown, creating a hair line typical of the Kayapó and of no other Amazonian tribe.

Anyway, getting back to the matter of the age of our oldest specimen, the trophy head probably dates back to the 1870s.

At first I thought we had acquired it through an exchange with a Brazilian museum, but Laila's search of our records disclosed that this prize object—quite possibly there may not be another one like it in this country—was donated to the Museum in 1877 by Earnest Morris, a man about whom we know nothing except his dates (1848-1880).

Our next oldest collection of objects is a small set of Karajá dolls, acquired through an exchange with the Museu Nacional in Rio de Janeiro, now sadly no longer in existence, having burned to the ground in a tragic fire last year. And what did the Brazilian museum receive from us in exchange for the Karajá dolls? Probably artifacts from the Northwest Coast or the Southwest, areas from which our collections were well supplied.

Karajá dolls are an item of great appeal to tourists. No better evidence of their popularity can be cited than that several years ago a couple of dozen Karajá dolls were placed on sale In an art gallery on Madison Avenue. With so many of these dolls in museums and in private collections, dolls that that had been collected over a period of more than a century, it is possible to see how these dolls have evolved over the years. The earlier forms, such as those we have on exhibit, are more elaborate than the later ones. Some of the older ones (although not ours) have wrap-around skirts made of banana leaves, which more recent ones lack.

The simplification that Karajá dolls have undergone is due, I suspect, to the fact that tourists, unaware that older dolls had more to them are ready to accept whatever is offered to them as traditional Karajá dolls.

Another important difference between the older ones—like those we have on display—and newer ones is that the older ones were unfired. Consequently they broke easily, and tourists began insisting on more durable ones. And since it was easy enough for the doll maker to put the dolls in the fire for a few minutes, baking them long enough to last longer, every doll made nowadays is probably baked hard.

Regardless of their age Karajá dolls are very distinctive. Nothing made anywhere in Amazonia that is at all like them. And, to the best of my knowledge, they continue to be high on the list of Amazonian souvenirs.

*   *   *   *

Not far from the Karajá dolls in the ceramics section of the hall are four large photographs showing various stages in the making of a pot, from shaping the clay to firing the vessel. These photos are one more example of how fellow Amazonianists have contributed to the enhancement of our hall. Warren Hern, the person who donated these photos of the ceramic art, has an M.D. degree as well as a Ph.D. in anthropology. And if one were awarded in photography, he would have that one too.

Several of his photographs have adorned calendars, a measure of how good he is with a camera.

I might well have introduced Warren earlier in this narrative when discussing puberty rituals and the pain they often cause the initiate. The only complaint I ever received about anything having to do with the South American hall came from a woman who ran a shelter for battered women. She had brought a number of women from the shelter to the Museum and when they walked through the "Life Cycle" section of the hall some of them were disturbed when they read about the practice of clitoridectomy among the Shipibo of the Peruvian Montaña. Dr. Hern, who as part of his field work among that tribe attends to their medical needs, routinely conducts pelvic examinations of the women. He told me that he had found evidence of clitoridectomy among older women of the tribe but that the Shipibo no longer practiced it.

* * * *

What I said earlier about the Mumdurucú head trophy was meant to serve as an introduction to a more extended discussion of Amazonian warfare. Having been sidetracked from that discussion I would like now to return to it.

Adjacent to the Mundurucú head is a woodcut taken from Hans Staden's *The True History of His Captivity,* first published in 1556. Staden was a German artilleryman in the employ of the Portuguese navy when, going ashore with a party of men to secure fresh water for the vessel, he was taken prisoner by the Tupinambá, a warlike tribe that lived along the coast of Brazil. In addition to their bellicosity, the Tupinambá were redoubtable cannibals. Staden's book describes his captivity among them during which he expected to be killed and eaten, almost from day to day. While awaiting his fate, Staden witnessed the eating of several other captives and, after escaping, he wrote the most detailed and authentic eye-witness account of cannibalism ever to appeared in print.

To add a touch of verisimilitude to our depiction of Tupinambá cannibalism we included in the warfare exhibit some woodcuts taken from Staden's book.

As highly practiced cannibals as the Tupinambá were, they were matched by the Caribs of the Lesser Antilles. In fact, the very word "cannibal" is derived from the word "Carib." To offer some evidence— perhaps a bit overblown—of the Island Caribs' refinement in the practice of cannibalism it was said that they could distinguish the taste of a Frenchman from that of a Spaniard, and both from that of a Dutchman.

Altogether we had enough credible detailed information about Amazonian cannibalism to have mounted a full blown exhibit on that subject had we wished to.

Our decision not to do so was based not on any excessive sensitivity on our part, however. We were fully ready to acknowledge the pervasiveness and importance of warfare and associated practices in Amazonia. War can be coldly and calmly analyzed. It was assuredly not the expression of the brimming over of an innate and irrepressible bloodlust. Warfare was rather the determinate and intelligible response by peoples to their circumstances. But our exhibit was not the place to launch into a broad gauged discussion of the causes of war. We felt we could deal with only certain aspects of it, cannibalism being one.

*   *   *   *

After these remarks, let us return narrowly to the grisly specifics of Amazonian warfare. Stepping back a few paces let us revisit the Kayapó warrior, standing there with his war club upraised, ready to dash out the brains of an enemy.

Quite a number of stories surround this Kayapó. The question is, where to begin?

First, I should point out that there are a dozen or more Kayapó villages, closely related to each other in language and culture but each one of them is politically autonomous —as is the rule throughout Amazonia.

The manikin in our exhibit is not meant to represent any particular Kayapó group but might be takem to stand for any one of them. Let us take a group which, before they became better known to outsiders were referred to as the Chukahamay. (I actually met one of them when I was in the Upper Xingú in 1953.) The name Chukahamay was not their own designation for themselves but was given to them by their enemies, the Juruna. It means "people without bows," which turned out to be a misnomer. Like all other Kayapó groups, the Chukahamay did indeed have bows, only they chose not to use them in warfare, preferring instead to employ war clubs. After clubbing an enemy to death with a club they laid it down next to his body, never to be used again.

Since the Chukahamay use their bows only for hunting and not for fighting, they gained the reputation among their enemies—who knew them only on the battlefield—of lacking the bow. The name therefor seemed appropriate enough.

With regard to the manikin, I might mention, in passing, how I struggled with posing the Kayapó warrior in such a way that he would not look as if he were stepping up to the plate with a baseball bat in his hands!

Once the Kayapó manikinwas finally posed, I needed to learn more about Kayapó warfare so I could say something accurate and informative about it to use as label copy. I decided to ask Joan Bamberger for some details about it since she had done field work among the Gorotire, a Kayapó group in central Brazil.

Joan, however, was reluctant to provide it, saying that the Kayapó she knew no longer engaged in warfare and that she preferred not to have that aspect of their culture appear to be the dominant thing about them.

Well, *bien entendu.*

But be that as it may, I still needed a label to place next to the manikin which said something of substance about the warrior's apparent readiness to use his war club. Shortly thereafter I happened to receive in the mail from Gustav Verswijver, a Belgian ethnologist who had done field work with a Kayapó group, a copy of his doctoral dissertation entitled *Kayapó Warfare*.

"My cup runeth over," I thought. We now had more than enough information to write a label for the manikin.

About this same time our manikin making was arousing considerable interest within the walls of theMuseum. Enough so that *Natural History*, then published by the Museum, decided to run an article about the procedure. They interviewed Laila about it since she had witnessed several manikins being made, the most recent one being that of the Kayapó warrior. Thus in describing in detail the making of that manikin she also gave an account of Kayapó warfare.

The issue of *Natural History* containing Laila's interview happened to fall into the hands of a woman in Laytonville, California, who wrote a letter to the editor of the magazine complaining about the portrayal of the Kayapó, saying that from all she knew about them they were a peaceful people of hunters and cultivators and objected to having them pictured in *Natural History* as warlike. The editor turned her letter over to me for reply. And fortunately, a few days earlier, I had received Verswijver's thesis on Kayapó warfare and was thus able to tell the woman that an anthropologist would hardly have written a 300-page dissertation on something that did not exist.

*   *   *   *

But there is more to the Kayapó story. A lot more.

Some time after the Kayapó manikin was in place but before the hall had been open to the public, Terrence Turner came to the Museum for a visit. As a married couple Terry and Joan Bamberger had done field work together among the Gorotire, which are, as I stated, a Kayapó sub-group. Now, however, they were divorced. I knew how Joan felt about our depiction of the Kayapó as warriors, but how would Terry feel about it?

The warfare section of the hall is about three-quarters of the way around from the introductory alcove so it took a while for Terry and me to get to it and as we walked along my anticipation mounted. When we finally reached the manikin I said nothing, waiting to hear Terry's reaction. He stood looking at the Kayapó warrior for a few seconds and then said,

"You know, that's just the way the Kayapó would like to be represented."

I didn't exactly breathe a sigh of relief, but I felt the satisfaction of having gotten it right.

*　　*　　*　　*

The Kayapó might have stopped fighting, as Joan said, but they were still tough guys, and wanted to be regarded as such.

In fact, not long after Terry's visit they took the president of FUNAI captive and held him hostage for a few days until FUNAI acceded to certain of their demands. How many other tribes would have dared to do such a thing?

However, returning to the Kayapó manikin once more, Terry noted that something was missing. The Kayapó, he said, usually wore armbands when they went on a war raid, but our manikin's arms were bare. "However," he added, "I think I can get a pair of them for you the next time I'm in Brazil. Would you like me to try?"

I jumped at the offer without really believing it would come to pass. A year or two later, though, after the South American hall had officially opened, I heard from Terry that he was coming to New York with a couple of Kayapó in tow and had something for me. I knew right away what that would be.

Then an idea came to me. Here was a chance for us to score some political points. Not long before this, NAGPRA had become the law of the land, and the repatriation of Indian artifacts from museums which had accepted federal funds was in full swing. Needless to say, that included us. To prepare for this, several persons had been added to the Anthropology department staff to work up inventories of our holdings of material from each of the more than 200 tribes recognized by the Bureau of Indian Affairs.

Especially vulnerable would be those artifacts which, because of their religious or ritual significance were candidates for repatriation. Then, with such lists in hand, the tribes would have an idea of just what objects of theirs they could ask to be returned to them.

I have never been a great friend of repatriation. However, I'm very much in favor of modern-day Indian tribes recalling and revivifying their traditional culture, and of our helping them to do so. But I would prefer to see this happen by having members of each tribe come to museums—ours included, of course—and spending time there carefully studying how their traditional artifacts were made so that they could faithfully duplicate them—and take pride in their ability to do so.

This would be better, it seemed to me, than having the tribes remove their artifacts from places where they had been securely housed and well curated for decades, only to be taken to where they might be properly looked after for a generation or two, but then what?

Now, thanks to Terry Turner, I saw the prospect of having South American Indians come to the Museum and actually reverse roles. Instead of taking something away from a museum they would be giving something to it.

Hoping to take advantage of this, I began carrying out my plan. I arranged for the large glass front of the Kayapó case to be temporarily removed so that the Indians accompanying Terry could step inside the case and slip the armbands onto the manikin.

Moreover, the removal of the glass front would make it easier to photograph the interior of the case since it would eliminate the reflection of the popping flash bulbs of the dozens of press photographers I hoped would be present at the occasion. I had asked the Public Affairs department to notify the media of the unusual occurrence that was to take place so that it could be recorded for posterity.

But it was not to be. in the immortal words of the Scottish poet Robert Burns, "The best laid plans of mice and men gang aft agley."

Highly anticipated by us, the great day arrived. But much to our chagrin and without giving us prior notice, the UN had gone ahead with their own plans. It was early in the fall and the annual opening session of the General Assembly was set to occur on that very day. It also happened to be the Day of the Child at the UN and to mark both occasions some thirty heads of state from around the world were to be in attendance.

And showing very little sense of proportion, the New York press and the rest of the media chose to cover the UN instead of us.

All told only one member of the press showed up at the Museum—a lonely reporter from the local Long Island newspaper *Newsday*. And he had the show all to himself.

One happy surprise, though, was in store for us. After slipping the armbands onto the manikin, one of the two Kayapó accompanying Terry suddenly zipped open the beach bag he had with him and pulled out a headdress of his own and proceeded to place it on the manikin.

So now we could be assured that the Kayapó warrior was ready to go into battle fully attired.

*   *   *   *

I have described the Kayapo's weapon as a war club, and so it was. But it also could serve a rather different function. The bellicosity that the Kaypó showed toward the outside world was sometimes turned inward. This happened when an internal dispute boiled over and the disputants, in an effort to resolve the issue, resorted to a serious form of dueling, with the club being the weapon of choice.

We did not have any way of showing Kayapó dueling but, curiously enough, a thousand miles to the north the Yanomamö engaged in a very similar type of dueling.

And, thanks to photographs and eye witness accounts of them by Napoleon Chagnon, we did have good material to show dueling—if not an actual duel in progress, at least the tangible results of one. And this evidence, mostly in the form of photographs, appears just to the right of the Kayapó warrior.

There are four stages to Yanomamö dueling, each one more violent than the previous one. The second one, which follows the first one, which consists of chest pounding, is carried out with clubs. The opponents stand facing each other and alternate hit each other on the head. Deep gashes in the scalp often result which, upon healing, leave conspicuous scars. These scars, clearly visible in Chagnon's photographs, are regarded as badges of fortitude and are proudly displayed, made especially prominent by tonsuring the head.

If these duels, which sometimes pit opposing factions against each other, do not succeed in resolving the issue, the result may be that the village splits into two. In that case one of the factions—usually the losing one— establishes a new village at some distance from the old.

* * * *

During the installation of the South American hall we had our own dispute within the Anthropology department, but hardly of the magnitude of those in a Yanomamö village. It arose over something not directly related to our hall, but which nonetheless had broad implications for anthropology halls in general. It began in the following way.

The Metropolitan Museum of Art, which for many years had shunned the art of preliterate peoples, had at last decided to venture into that field. In that connection they were putting on a temporary exhibit on the art of the Maori of New Zealand. The exhibit was about to open, and the Met had invited several Maori elders to come from New Zealand to be present at the event. The Met's opening coincided with an advanced stage in the reinstallation of our Pacific hall. Included in this hall were a number of Maori objects, the most prominent of which were some examples of Maori tattooing, an art at which the Maori were unsurpassed.

Maori tattooing was best exemplified on trophy heads—heads taken as an adjunct of warfare, which was frequent and intense among the Maori. It is my understanding that Maori heads are not uncommon in major museum collections, which is not surprising since the Maori were almost constantly at war, thus providing their tattoo artists with ample material to work with.

Unbeknownst to us in the Anthropology department, Malcolm Arth, head of our Education department, fad taken the liberty of inviting the Maori elders, who were already in New York for the Met opening, to come to the American Museum to see how Maori culture was being portrayed in our not-yet-open Pacific hall. The elders came and, according to reports, though they made no big fuss about it, were not pleased to see Maori trophy heads so liberally on view. (As I recall, we had seven or eight of them in the exhibit.) And they made their displeasure known to Museum authorities.

Although I had no direct involvement in any of this, it nevertheless gave me pause. And while I never mentioned it to anyone, in private I wondered if the real reason the Maori elders objected to seeing all those trophy heads on display was having Museum visitors see with what reckless abandon their ancestors lopped off human heads.

The issue of the Maori heads came to the attention of the director of the American Museum, who said, very properly,

"All right, Anthropology, this is your problem. You deal with it."

And so we had a departmental meeting to consider the matter. After much discussion we voted to remove the Maori heads from the exhibit.

I strongly objected to this but was outvoted.

Suspecting that my theory about the real reason for the Maoris' objection to our exhibiting the heads might be true, I suggested that we reduce the number of heads we were exhibiting from seven or eight to just two or three. Moreover, I proposed that we add more information on the process of tattooing which, after all, was the point of the exhibit. That would perhaps have deflected a bit of the spotlight away Maori warfare and the multiple decapitations of corpses that followed it.

Thus I was ready to accede somewhat to what I call institutional squeamishness, which I thought we might be showing.

To give another example of what I mean by this let me cite another exhibit in the new Pacific hall—an example which, in all likelihood, was being carried over, unmodified, from the old one. A small exhibit case was devoted to Fijian culture in which one see a tiny artifact correctly identified as a "cannibal fork." Yet nary a word was said in that case about Fijian warfare, which, for the winning side, culminated in a cannibalistic feast. The existence of cannibal forks provided indisputable evidence, not only of Fijian warfare, but of their having carried cannibalism to a high culinary art.

But let us go back to the Maori heads. Initially, as I indicated, my arguments proved unavailing, but I kept at it informally. And a second departmental meeting was held on the subject and his time we voted to keep the trophy heads on display. I had won, it seemed, but my victory was short lived.

A third meeting was held on the matter, this time in the Pacific hall itself, with the participants in it being expanded to include the head of the Education department, the head of Public Affairs, the director of the Museum, and others. The issue of the Maori heads was argued up, down, and sideways, the upshot being that the heads were to be removed from exhibition altogether.

As a result of this vote, no vestige remains in the Pacific hall of Maori tattooing, an art at which they were probably the best in the world.

Having lost the vote on the Maori heads, I put my colleagues on notice that when it came to tackling the warfare section of the South American hall, Jívaro shrunken heads would appear in it without apology. Furthermore, the reasons behind the shrinking of enemy heads and the technique of doing so would be explained in full detail.

And indeed, to jump ahead of the story, there is a small, stand-alone case in the warfare section devoted solely to Jívaro head shrinking. And I might add that in the twenty years between the hall's opening and my retirement as Curator of South American Ethnology the number of complaints I received from the supposedly sensitive public about the trophy heads was … none.

But staying on the subject of shrunken heads, the question remains, what if the Jívaro had asked to have their *tsantsas* repatriated? What would my response have been?

I had thought about this long and hard. In the first place, I would have pointed out to them that the repatriation act—NAGPRA—applied only to Indian tribes residing within the United States. Thus an Ecuadorian tribe would have no legal claim under its provisions.

But even without having the law on their side the Jívaro might still have asked for the heads to be returned. What would I have said to them then?

That became more of a possibility, I thought, when I learned a few years later that a group of Jívaro (Shuar, remember) had been brought to New York from Ecuador by Steve Rubenstein, an ethnologist who had studied them in the field, and that they would be visiting the Museum. I happened to be out of town during their visit so I didn't have a chance to meet them, but in answer to the question of questions I would have said, speaking through Steve, who knew their language:

"If anyone should get these heads back it shouldn't be you, but the Achuar, your historic enemies, whose heads they most surely were."

But I didn't have a chance to say this, nor would there have been a need to do so, for as Steve told me later, the Jívaro made no such request. Indeed, they were pleased with the way we had presented an important aspect of their traditional culture.

*   *   *   *

Now, by way of contrast, let me describe how my feeling about the shrunken heads differed from that of the Museum of the American Indian under their new leadership.

One day I received a phone call from Nancy Rosoff, my counterpart at the MAI, inviting me to help her go through their collection of heads, separating the genuine specimens from the fakes. Having had some experience at this, I was ready to accept her invitation.

The separation was to take place in the Annex of the MAI, located in the east Bronx. When I arrived there Nancy had already laid out on a large table some three dozen shrunken heads. Without further ado we proceeded to examine the heads, one by one, sorting them into two groups, one containing the genuine ones (by far the smaller pile) and the other containing the fakes.

After a while it became evident that Nancy could distinguish the real ones from the fakes about as well as I could, so I asked her, what was I doing there.

She explained that the new MAI administration had decided to take the genuine *tsantsas*, once they had been well authenticated, to some place in upstate New York and given a proper burial!

What could I possibly say to her that she, a sensible woman, probably wasn't thinking herself?

In the end, though, the genuine heads were not buried—in upstate New York or anywhere else. Instead, they were sent back to the Jívaro in Ecuador who placed them on exhibit in a small museum of their own that they had recently opened somewhere in the jungles of eastern Ecuador—not far, no doubt, from the very spot where the heads were originally severed and shrunk. Thus anyone who missed seeing them during their being on exhibit in New York, but still curious to lay eyes on them, coulg do so by expending a bit more effort than it would have taken when they were in residence here.

*   *   *   *

As the South American hall neared completion, the question arose, What were we going to name it? As long as we continued to work on it, we referred to it simply as the South American Hall. But now that it was on the verge of opening, we needed a formal name for it, one that I hoped would indicate precisely the nature of its contents.

During the installation process I kept my fingers crossed that some wealthy man, seeking to carve out a sliver of immortality for himself, would not come forward with a donation of ten million dollars to the Museum toward the construction of the hall with the expectation that it would be named after him. The last thing I wanted to see was the fruits of our nine years of labor crowned with the title of "The Frederick J. Funkhouse III Hall of South American Indians"—or something of the sort.

Fortunately, that never happened. The hall was built entirely with grant money plus some of the Museum's own funds. Still, a suitable name for it had to be chosen. The name "Hall of South American Peoples" was proposed but I didn't care for it. I preferred "Native Cultures of South America." After all, what we were exhibiting was not people—living and breathing human beings with black hair and brown skin—but their handiwork, their *culture*. Moreover, we were not exhibiting contemporary Indian culture (as the MAI chose to do), heavily overlaid as it was with so many elements of Western civilization.

Other names for the hall were proposed, debated, and rejected.

But alas, as I might well have done, I didn't push hard enough for my preference, which, after all, was easily the most appropriate designation we could have given it, for it indicated just what the hall actually contained.

And so the hall came to bear—and will no doubt continue to do so—the name of "The Hall of South American Peoples."

Nonetheless, misnomer though it may be, it still labels an exhibit hall which, to the best of our ability, presents the traditional life ways –the native cultures—of the peoples who inhabit and are adapted to the greatest expanse of rainforest on earth.

And there is a lot more ….